THE PERFECT FIT

A Woman's Look at the Armor of God

Mona L. Mauro

Get dressed.
Stand ready.
Dance Victoriously!

Beyond Blessed,
Mona
1/17

xulon
PRESS

The Perfect Fit
A Woman's Look At the Armor of God
by Mona L Mauro

Printed in the United States of America.

ISBN 9781498485708

All interior artwork by Mallory Beth Robbins

www.xulonpress.com

The Perfect Fit–Dedication

To Mom and Dad – Eleanor and John Gale

Mom, You showed me how to …
Unconditionally love others,
With gratitude, enjoy thoroughly the simple things in life,
Be involved in ministry, for the sake of the gospel,
Sing, no matter the circumstance,
Pray without ceasing, and live everyday sacrificially in response
To God's remarkable love for us.

Dad, You showed me how to …
Love deeply and say it,
Be faithful, trustworthy, and strong, work hard and figure it out,
Be true to my word, Put Family first,
Fish–for fish …And eventually, for so much more.

After I worship our Savior for a hundred years in Heaven,
you will definitely be the next ones I long to see.
Even now, I am looking forward to that embrace.
I love and miss you … every day..

The Perfect Fit

Table of Contents

WEEK ONE

Day One – Beyond Blessed

Day Two – I t's Good to be Alive

Day Three – Mystery Solved

Day Four – Gifts Galore and Clean Underwear

Day Five – Closet Cleaning

Sharpen Your Sword for Week One

Week One Wrap Up

WEEK TWO

Day One – Finally

Day Two – Get Dressed

Day Three – Why Can't I Stay in my PJs all day?

Day Four – Discussion in the Heavenlies

Day Five – An Evil Day

Sharpen Your Sword for Week Two

Week Two Wrap Up

WEEK THREE

Day One – Spiritually Standing

Day Two – Gird Your Waist

Day Three – A Woman of Integrity

Day Four – God is Truth

Day Five – What is Truth?

Sharpen Your Sword for Week Three

Week Three Wrap Up

WEEK FOUR

Day One – Breastplate of Righteousness

Day Two – Protect My Heart

Day Three – The Best We Can

Day Four – Righteousness – He's Doing His Best

Day Five – My Breastplate of Righteousness

Sharpen Your Sword for Week Four

Week Four Wrap Up

WEEK FIVE

Day One – Shoe Shopping

Day Two – Prepared to Share

Day Three – A Bounce in Your Step

Day Four – Wanna Hear Some Good News?

Day Five – My Shoes of Peace

Sharpen Your Sword for Week Five

Week Five Wrap Up

WEEK SIX

Day One – Above All, Take the Shield

Day Two – Enlisted into the Lord's Army & Ready to Fight

Day Three – Faith That My Father Knows Best

Day Four – Fiery Darts

Day Five – My Shield of Faith

Swords from the Armory-

Worry   *Fear   *Anxiousness

Hurting

Finances

Hope   *Peace   *Courage   *Faith

Healing

Addiction   *Struggle   *Defeat   *Sin

About the Author

Mona L Mauro

*M*ona is a teacher – from the top of her head to the tips of her toes. She passionately loves learning, sees lessons daily in life and feels compelled to share with any soul within hearing distance. Mona believes that teaching is her God-given gift, her calling and a passion that rules her life, especially when teaching God's Word to women. It is one of her greatest desires to see women living abundant lives, the lives Christ intended. She has been leading women's events – seminars, workshops, retreats, luncheons, classes and camps, for nearly 20 years ... loving every single moment. Her events are full of sincerity, relatable music, rich Biblical application, unforgettable object lessons and laughter – loud, contagious, eye-rolling laughter.

She and her husband, Paul, reside in southern New Jersey where they are devoted to family. They have three adult daughters, one son-in-law and a little dog, with big-attitude, named Bella. Mona enjoys teaching, researching topics, being outside and happy dancing.

Mona has a B.S. from Messiah College, several educational certifications, and is currently completing her masters from Rowan University. She has taught K-12 students, college students, college professors, and currently spends her days with middle school students.

About the Artist

Mallory Beth Robbins

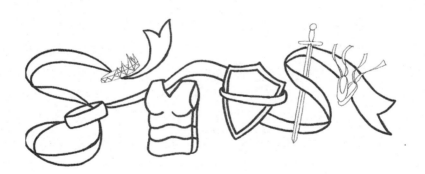

allory has always enjoyed art. She shares, "As a kid, my mom and I would color for hours, sometimes quietly, sometimes talking. When I paint or draw there is a quietness that surrounds me and I feel at peace. I am able to block out everything around me and relax. Recently, as I have been learning to Bible journal with art, it's been more like praying." Mallory would like to dedicate all the art work in **The Perfect Fit** to Eleanor C Robbins, her "Mum Mum," who touched many lives with her compassion and dedication to Jesus and God.

Acknowledgements from the Author

To the Ladies Sunday School Class of CCC–As quickly as I could write, you so graciously accepted these "naked pictures of myself." Your hunger for Truth, love for one another and willingness to learn taught me life lessons that I will forever treasure. Thank you.

To my Monday Night Ladies -Your honesty, diligence and heart inspire me. I am honored to call you my sisters and beyond blessed to do life with you.
Thank you for loving me, just as I am.

To my sisters, El & Gladys, and all of my other *sisters* that edited, read, reread, prayed over, responded and helped with this study – I have run out of words to express my gratitude. Your faithfulness, love and encouragement will forever be engraved on my heart and hidden between the lines. You kept me going and, once again, I thank you.

Andrea, Samantha and Michaela–I cherish and love you each "more than you'll ever know."
It is the desire of my heart to be a true woman of God before you, in every possible situation.
Thank you for keeping me real.

Paul–I fell in love with Jesus, before I fell for you over 30 years ago. I continue to fall daily for you both. Your discipline, faithfulness and love ground me and give me roots to grow deeper still. I love growing old with you. Thank you for giving me the freedom to be myself.

And, Father God, I told You I wasn't a writer, yet You continued to whisper in my heart that I should share. So, here it is and it is all Yours. Please use it as only You can. I am so humbled. Thanks for asking. I love You deeply and live daily to bring You glory…only You.

The Perfect Fit

A Woman's Look at the Armor of God

An Introduction

*I*t is with tremendous humility I share this study. Fear? Plenty. God's Word is precious to me. The thought of writing my personal insights concerning it is overwhelming. It is life-giving and tremendously personal. And yet, I strongly sense God's leading to read, pray, meditate, teach, write and share. So, with fear and trepidation, I obey … again.

Nine years ago I completed **The Perfect Fit** – *A Woman's Look at the Armor of God*. I reluctantly shared it with the group of women I was teaching and then … life got busy. In the busy came responsibilities and situations that caused me to put this and all writing away. Until now, nine years later.

Life has changed and so have I. Our three beautiful daughters, our gifts from God, were then all teenagers and at home. Today they are all in their twenties, finding their way and becoming best friends. I now have a son-in-law whom I adore. I enjoyed spending time with my parents who then lived nearby, now they are both in Heaven—after six challenging years of declining health. I was a part-time teacher in a Christian School; now, I am a fulltime teacher in Public School. My family was an active part of a small community church, now we fellowship with hundreds and hundreds. Seasons come and go; with each changing season we are forced to grow.

Thank God, some things have remained constant. I am pleased I have the same loving husband who puts up with me and clings to the heart-of-God. Miraculously, God continues to provide opportunity for me to teach His Word to women. (I am still incredibly humbled by each divine-appointment.) I remain blessed to be a part of a large growing family with lots of siblings, nieces and nephews that I love to pieces. And, best of all, God's love, mercy, peace and grace has remained steadfast. He is my firm foundation, my refuge, my Savior. Although my body has fluctuated over the years, the armor of God, full of power and life, remains a perfect fit.

Please know, through the initial writing process, I learned enormously. God seemed to take me through the Word, word-by-word, trial-by-trial, before He allowed me to share any part of it. It was a sort of *on the job training*. It would be absolutely impossible to be filled with pride during the writing, teaching and sharing. Gloriously, impossible. As I have examined the Word, trust me, it examined me. Recently I started at Ephesians 1:1, re-reading, re-visiting, again listening to God's heart, and I continue to learn that I have so much to learn.

I offer "**The Perfect Fit** – *A Woman's Look at the Armor of God*" to you sincerely from my humbled heart with this prayer for both of us: that God will open our eyes to His life-changing Truth, that we will intentionally fall in love with Jesus in a new way daily, and that we will learn how to fight the battles of life fully dressed in the magnificent, perfectly-fitted armor of God. We are His workmanship, created to live abundantly. Let's woman-up. Let's use the powerful weapons He has given us, trust our Commander-and-Chief, and live our lives victoriously. What an adventure lies ahead. Let's get dressed piece by piece by piece!

Beyond Blessed,
Mona L. Mauro

Family Photo

Study Notes–How to get the most out of this study

The Perfect Fit is designed for both personal study and group discussion. Ideally, you would gather a few girlfriends together for a ten-session, nine week in-depth Bible study of Ephesians, especially Ephesians 6:10-20. Pray about this adventure, commit to meeting together and learn how to daily get dressed in the full armor of God.

First, **The Perfect Fit** includes personal interactive lessons designed to enrich your learning and application of Scripture. The objective is that through your completion of the written work in this workbook, Days one through five each week, the Holy Spirit would use your efforts toward victorious living. Don't be intimidated by the homework, just do your best, and be faithful. God will bless your efforts.

Second, to enrich your group time, prepare the Principal Question of the Day and the Question for Personal Application. Your small group will likely discuss these questions during your time together, as well as complete your Session of the Week. You will not be required to share your answers unless you desire. Oh, how I wish I could be personally present with you at each weekly gathering. Work together on memorizing Ephesians 6:10-20.

Each day as you study individually you will see the following symbols.

A Principal Question of the Day

This starburst represents a question about a passage directly related to the day's study that you should be ready to discuss in your weekly meeting time. It is a principal concept and important.

A Question for Personal Application.

This smiling face represents a question about personal application directly related to the day's study that you might be willing to share in your weekly meeting time.

Weekly Wrap Up

At the end of each week is a compilation of each day's written work questions for group review.

Sharpen Your Sword for each Week

At the end of each week there is a page called "Sharpen Your Sword." Record prayer requests that come up that week. (If you already have a prayer journal that you use consistently, then feel free to continue.) It is important that you briefly write the request(s) followed by a short phrase from a scripture truth, promise of God, Sword of the Spirit with reference. <u>This is such a crucial step in learning how to use the Sword of the Spirit in the battles of life</u>. You may always choose a verse from the day's lesson, one you already know or look up one in the topical reference guide in the back of "The Perfect Fit." Date each entry. As you see God at work answering your prayers, be sure to return to that page and note the answer.

Memorizing and Meditating–Ephesians 6:10-20

Just like soldiers learn to discipline themselves to be fully prepared for battle, the daily practice of learning Ephesians 6:10-20 will be training for your mind. Please, I beg of you, do not skip this crucial step. Do not start the study believing the lie that you are not able to memorize Ephesians 6:10-20. You would be surrendering to the enemy without even a fight. With discipline, review, hard-work and the power of God, you are able to memorize most, if not all. Many soldier sisters before you have taken this challenge and surprised themselves at the end with the ability to quote from memory many verses. I smile at the thought!

At the end of each day's lesson, you will see the heart symbol. This is a reminder to continue reviewing Ephesians 6:10-20. The memory work begins with one verse and adds weekly. I have included tricks and tips to help you with this task. At the end, if you have only memorized six verses instead of ten, celebrate those six powerful verses engraved on your heart. I know you will use them to defeat the enemy, in the name and power of Jesus. Fight on!

Session of the Week – Your Strategic Planning Meeting

At the beginning of each week's study there is a "Session of the Week". This is meant to introduce you to the next week's verse and content. If you have a facilitator or leader, they may guide you through this overview. The answers are in the back, "Suggested Answers for Session of the Week."

"Session for Week #10", the Soldier Sister Celebration is a culmination of study. So, plan a party. Invite guests. Enjoy theme related foods. Be creative and have a blast. I so desire to join in on your festivity, please be sure to take a photo and send it to me. With your permission, I will be happy to post on my website.

Following these guidelines will provide you will the tools needed to complete **The Perfect Fit**.

Memorization of Ephesians 6:10-20 (NKJV)

In effort to memorize Ephesians 6:10-20, we will work on it weekly. By constantly reviewing, the passage will be yours to use as a weapon against the enemy. With discipline and determination, in God's power, you can do this. I know you can!

Week #1

[10]Finally, my brethren, be strong in the Lord and in the power of His might. [11]Put on the whole armor of God, that you may be able to stand against the wiles of the devil.

Week #2

[12]For we do not wrestle against flesh and blood, but against principalities, against powers, against the rulers of the darkness of this age, against spiritual *hosts* of wickedness in the heavenly *places.* [13]Therefore take up the whole armor of God, that you may be able to withstand in the evil day, and having done all, to stand.

Week #3

[14]Stand therefore, having girded your waist with truth,

Week #4

Having put on the breastplate of righteousness,

Week #5

[15]and having shod your feet with the preparation of the gospel of peace.

Week #6

[16]above all, taking the shield of faith with which you will be able to quench all the fiery darts of the wicked one.

Week #7

[17]And take the helmet of salvation,

Week #8

and the sword of the Spirit, which is the word of God;

Week #9

[18]praying always with all prayer and supplication in the Spirit, being watchful to this end with all perseverance and supplication for all the saints-[19]and for me, that utterance may be given to me, that I may open my mouth boldly to make known the mystery of the gospel, [20]for which I am an ambassador in chains; that in it I may speak boldly, as I ought to speak.

The Perfect Fit

Session #1 – Overview of Ephesians 1:1-6:9

We are building a _____ on which to stand dressed in the full armor of God.

Paul, author of Ephesians, was a _____.

Who we are and what we have in Christ:

B–We are _____ Ephesians 1

A–We are _____ Ephesians 2

M–We are a part of the _____ Ephesians 3

G–We've been given _____ Ephesians 4

O–We are to discard sin," _____, in with the new". Ephesians 5

R–We are to trust the Holy Spirit in our _____. Ephesians 6:1-9

Ephesians 6:10-11

Finally, my brethren, be strong in the Lord and in the power of His might.

Put on the whole armor of God,

that you may be able to stand against the wiles of the devil.

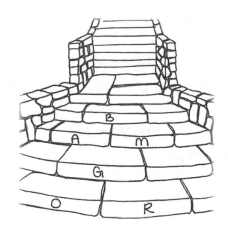

The Perfect Fit

Week One   Day One

Beyond Blessed!

"Blessed be the God and Father of our Lord Jesus Christ, who has blessed us with every spiritual blessing in the heavenly places in Christ, just as He chose us in Him before the foundation of the world, that we should be holy and without blame before Him in love..."
Ephesians 1:3-4

I have heard it said that some beginning a new novel read the ending before they begin the book. Personally, I can't understand that. Where's the intrigue? The suspense? They are probably the same people who like to know what's *in* the wrapped present before they open it. The passage containing the full armor of God is at the end of the book of Ephesians. You already know how the book ends! So for those *Eager Enders*, let's begin in Chapter 1 so we can better understand the ending.

Biblical scholars believe that the book of Ephesians was written by the apostle Paul while he was imprisoned in Rome in approximately 60 AD. (Paul's story of his faith in Christ is told in Acts 9. It's a tremendous story; I would suggest you read it if you are not familiar with it.) He was being held captive because of his boldness in sharing the gospel of Jesus Christ. It was during this trial that he penned this book. Paul was quite familiar with the city of Ephesus and the Ephesians that lived there. He visited Ephesus at the end of his second missionary journey.

This week we will set a foundation of six bricks to stand upon as a woman dressed in the full armor of God. Each foundational brick will be a chapter or section in Ephesians 1-6:10. We will use the acronym "B.A.M.G.O.R." to assist in our foundational place to stand. Let's begin by reading Ephesians 1:1-3.

Paul introduces himself, addresses his readers, gives a greeting and then blows us away right from the start.

What does he write in verse three concerning his readers?

Here's our "B" for Ephesians 1 – Blessings! We open the Book and immediately are reminded that we have been blessed in Christ with every spiritual blessing in the heavenly places.
Write what you think a few of the spiritual blessings might be.

 Like that's not enough, continue reading in Ephesians 1:4-14.
List some of the blessings mentioned in this passage.

If I were to ask you to list your blessings, logically, family, friends, home and belongings may be the first things you mention. Although they *are* blessings from God, each can be taken from us without notice. Fire, flood, death, and other tragedies can remove these blessings.

If that were to happen, would we still be blessed?

The world, schedules, time restraints, trials and life itself seem to crowd our thinking and we *forget* how truly blessed we are. It is then we need to practice *The Pause*. Stressed? *Pause.* Fearful? *Pause.* Worried? *Pause*, praise and remember our many rich blessings from God. Our identity. Our calling. Who He says we are. When our *blessings list* begins with those mentioned in Ephesians 1:4-14, then our priorities are in order. The blessing that "God has chosen us" (v. 4), and that "He made us accepted in the Beloved" (v. 6) cannot be taken from us. The blessings that we, as believers, "should be to the praise of His glory" (v. 12). These cannot be removed by fire, flood or any catastrophe this world affords.

We need to practice 'The Pause.'	Read Romans 8:37-39. What are we according to verse 37? In reading Romans 8:38-39, nothing can separate us from what? Is that a blessing? How?

Knowing our spiritual blessings and placing them on the top of our *blessings list* does great things to the way we wear the full armor of God. We walk in confidence when we are secure in the love God has given us. We hold our head high when we understand that "God has chosen us." When we know, I mean really KNOW, "He made us accepted in the Beloved" we trust Him to "work all things out together for good." We are soldiers wearing the full armor with complete trust in our Commander-In-Chief. We walk sure-footed and are able to fight the "fiery darts of the wicked."

But I'm getting ahead of myself, let's continue in Ephesians 1:14. This is our inheritance and we must live daily knowing it is true. Because it is. Do you believe it?

How do we live daily knowing it is true? Take a moment to thank God for these blessings which have been lavished upon us. (Go ahead.)

 List 3 spiritual blessings that you are certain of in your personal life.

We could take all week to examine each blessing mentioned but time and space will not permit. Yet, just for fun, let's look specifically at "adoption of sons" (or we could say *daughters*). In this case *adoption* refers to a Roman custom by which a person not having children of his own might adopt as his son one born of other parents. The relationship was, for all intents and purposes, the same that existed between a natural father and son.

I had the opportunity to be a witness during court proceedings when dear friends adopted a seven-year-old Russian boy. Not only was I honored to be a witness that day, I will forever treasure the statements made by the judge. He said, "This child has all rights and privileges of a biological child, even to the point of inheritance." As a mother, I thought of this young boy's biological mother. This Russian woman had absolutely no rights to this boy's life. She birthed this sweet child, he shared her DNA and features, yet she had no say in any part of his life.

What does Colossians 1:12 say about our part in the inheritance of the saints?

We are born in sin. In our own strength—we sin. (Personally, I can tell you... EVERY TIME.) If left to our own *nature,* we will sin. Yet, the Father adopts us as His own and we have all rights as His child. Do I hear an "Amen?"

What are some of your rights as a biological or adopted earthly family member?

(Example: intimate conversation)

Compare this to our heavenly Father. What are some *rights* you have with Him because you have been adopted?

In case you were not able to begin imagining the blessings we possess, because of our relationship with Jesus, check out these verses and write in the privileges/blessings we have as children of God. Remember, this is just a few...

Romans 5:2 _____

Hebrews 7:25-26 _____

John 17:2 _____

2 Peter 1:4 _____

Paul loved the Gentile believers in Ephesus and desired that they enjoy victorious lives in Christ. With this letter, he wanted to encourage and equip them to live lives that glorified God. So, he prayed for them.

Read Ephesians 1:15-23.

He prayed, first, that they would have "the spirit of wisdom and revelation"; second, that their "eyes of understanding would be enlightened"; third, that they may know what is the "hope of His calling and riches of His glory" and fourth, that they would "know exceeding greatness of power toward other believers." Now there is a prayer *packed with a punch*–the actual POWER of God.

As we begin this study together, let's use Paul's prayer as a pattern to pray for God's blessing for our understanding of Ephesians and, in particular, of the putting on the full armor of God (Ephesians 6:10-18).

Our Precious Father,

We come to you humbly in your Son Jesus' name and we ask that you would give to us the Spirit of wisdom and revelation in the knowledge of Jesus as we study Your Word. Open our eyes of understanding that we may know the hope we have as Your child. Help us to catch a glimpse of the riches of the glory of the inheritance we have as your daughters.

Fill us with the exceeding greatness of Your power so we may live, as you desire. We understand it is only in Your strength that we can walk victoriously. Amen

Turn to the **Sharpen Your Sword for Week One** and be sure to write a verse to correlate.

Be sure to begin studying for memorization Ephesians 6:10. Write it and treasure each word.

The Perfect Fit

Week One   Day Two

"It's Good to Be Alive!"

"And you He made alive, who were dead in trespasses and sins, in which you once walked according to the course of this world, according to the prince of the power of the air, the spirit who now works in the sons of disobedience..." Ephesians 2:1-2

"It's great to be alive.
Wide awake in time.
I'm looking at the world and now I'm not afraid to let my faith arise.
I believe, this is the day, that the Lord has made.
So open up your eyes
Be taken by surprise, it's great to be alive!"

*B*abbie Mason wrote these beautiful lyrics and they make me smile every time I hear them. They came to my mind as I read chapter two of Ephesians. It begins with the incredible words "He made us alive." YES! (Repeat that with great excitement even with an arm in the air, if you dare.) I'm alive. Alive!! Here is our "A" for Ephesians two – Alive.

According to Ephesians 2:1-2, what were we dead in?
We fulfilled the desires of _____.

What are some of the desires of your flesh? (Things that you feel in bondage to ... Food? Fear? Worry? Family?)

Read Ephesians 2:4-10.

In verse four Paul begins with "But God." In our selfish thinking, in our pride... we were dead in our sins but God turned the whole thing around. He is rich in _____ and great _____. He accepted our dead, sinful selves and made us _____ in Christ through grace.

Not only are we alive in Christ, no longer dead to ourselves and our sin, but according to Ephesians 2:6, what else is part of this incredible package?

In week six we'll be discussing faith in detail but we must understand that the truth–this *alive-ness*–we have rights to, is graciously granted to us only because of our faith in Christ.

What must one do to receive this promised *alive-ness*?

This could be considered a trick question because actually we can do nothing to receive it. What could we possible do to obtain God's grace? It is totally a gift from Him. We only need to believe. So what do we *believe*? Read Ephesians 2:11-13. (Go ahead. Be reminded.)

Verse eleven suggests we remember that at one time we were without Christ having no hope and without God. Verse thirteen awakens us again with "But now." We were dead... NOW ALIVE. We were lost and far off, but now have been brought near by the blood of Christ.

 What does it mean <u>to you</u> to be "alive with Christ."
Does this fact affect your everyday living?

 According to 1 Peter 3:18, what are we alive to? And how did this take place?

What does it mean to be alive with Him according to Colossians 2:13-14?

I do not possess a *green thumb,* but from my childhood I can always remember our home being flooded with beautiful healthy green houseplants. Ivy, African violets, spider plants, and the like, would hang from my mother's front bay window. I love houseplants but I must confess that my children will have no such memory. Why? Because I do not care for my houseplants as I should. They *look* alive atop my shelf, but because I do not fertilize, talk to them (;-) or even water them, they are dead. Their roots are just under the surface and often they look wilted. Eventually, the plant will die and be discarded.

Without Christ, we are dead. We have no roots or any appearance of life in us, it is just a facade. We can *look* alive. We may even know some religious verbiage or Christian lingo... but we are dead. We may even go to church, sing in the choir, talk the talk but if the Spirit of God is not alive in us and flowing through us we, like my sad little plants, we are really dead.

Once we accept the *life* God offers us through Christ… once we acknowledge our need for redemption and surrender our lives to His will for us… once we, by faith, accept Christ's death on the cross as payment for our sin… my sin (it's personal), your sin… we are given life. REAL LIFE. The abundant life as spoken of in John 10:10.

Write John 10:10.

> ... to be
> **truly alive**
> **with purpose**
> **and calling**.

Once we are saved by faith, accepting Jesus as our Savior from our sin, the blessings and abundant life are ours. Obviously, this doesn't mean we will have a trouble-free life but it does mean that we have His promise to never leave us alone. His Spirit will guide us when we are surrendered to Him through all the valleys of life. This is life at its best.

To remain spiritually alive I must remember from where God has brought me. I was once dead in my sins. I wanted my own way and justified my sins with excuses. I remember behaving contrary to God's Word and justifying the reasons for my choices. I was so full of pride and self-righteousness. The Holy Spirit spoke to my heart and I realized the bondage I was in. I was in the wrong place, at the wrong time, with the wrong people, far from God.

I asked for forgiveness and, by faith, accepted Christ as my Savior. I still struggle with being obedient to the Word but now I make the daily choice to be cleansed of sin. I must die to myself, Mona's will, and surrender to what God has brought into my life. I must be watered by the Spirit, through His Word, so my roots can be nourished then growth can really occur.

Read Ephesians 2:14-18. Here we are reminded that He, Jesus Christ Himself, is our _____.

It is through His death on the cross that peace has been made with God. We have peace *with* God, which gives us the peace *of* God. (In week 5, we'll discuss peace extensively.)

Finally, to wrap up the second chapter of Ephesians, what are a few truths we reminded of in verses 19-22?

How does knowing these truths, that we are not alone and that there is a greater plan, encourage us to be alive in Christ?

Not just breathing, working, and living, but to be truly *alive* with purpose and calling. That is abundant living and where we begin getting dressed in the pieces of the armor of God.

It <u>is</u> good to be alive!

 Write prayer requests that are on your mind today on **Sharpen Your Sword for Week One**. Be sure to include verses you can claim as yours while you pray.

 Continue to memorize Ephesians 6:10. Write it on the lines below.

_____

_____

Write what this verse means to you personally today.

The Perfect Fit

Week One   Day Three

Mystery Solved!

"For this reason I bow my knees to the Father of our Lord Jesus Christ, from whom the whole family in heaven and earth is named, that He would grant you, according to the riches of His glory, to be strengthened with might through His Spirit in the inner man, that Christ may dwell in your hearts through faith; that you, being rooted and grounded in love, may be able to comprehend with all the saints what is the width and length and depth and height – to know the love of Christ which passes knowledge; that you may be filled with all the fullness of God."
Ephesians 3:14-19

As I sort the third load of laundry of the day, I realize I am missing three socks: one blue striped, one red and a pink *Princess* sock. I am convinced they went into the washer and into the dryer, but somewhere in between a great mystery evolved. At this moment–they have disappeared. I did not even have to say "Abracadabra!" Their matches have vanished.

Ephesians Chapter Three solves a great mystery and God chose Paul, a Jew who had at one time martyred those in the early church, to reveal His truth to the non-Jews, Gentiles. Here is our "M" – Mystery. It is interesting to me that a Jew was chosen because this mystery involves the gentiles. Through history, the Messiah was promised to the Jews. They were God's chosen people. But when Christ came he said, "Whosoever may come." He invited us all–that includes you and me... Gentile and Jew.

Understanding our redemption in Christ, Chapter one, and the *aliveness* we have in God, Chapter 2, is sometimes hard to believe. So Paul explains this mystery of God in Chapter three. Read slowly and deliberately Ephesians three for understanding. Pray for comprehension.

Did you read the entire chapter? _____ What is the mystery revealed?

A mystery is a plan or a story with parts unrevealed. This is God's wise plan that was previously hidden, but now made clear and available to all.

Explain the mystery revealed in verse six?

The term *fellow heirs* invites us all; we are all one body. The Jews were chosen, but we are also included. We share the inheritance equally.

 What do you think is part of this *inheritance*?
Have you ever inherited anything? If so, what?
How did it make you feel to be included?

When I think of who I am ... When I consider my pride, bad attitude, selfishness, and sin, I am amazed to be included in the inheritance of God.

Read Ephesians 3:8-9. How did Paul feel about his place?

To Paul, it was a mystery to be included in this Great Mystery.
According to 8-13, what is the purpose of this mystery?

Because of Jesus, even we Gentiles, who were once "far off," now have "boldness and access the throne of God with confidence" through our faith in Him. (Ephesians 3:12)

The apostle Paul begins this third chapter in response to chapters one and two. He then continues on a discourse about this *mystery* and our place in it. Finally, in Ephesians 3:14 it seems he gets back to the reason for his writing. He revealed the mystery in verses 1-7, gave the purpose of the mystery in verses 8-13 and now he states the appreciation for the mystery in verses 14-21. Try to comprehend the mystery revealed and our amazing place in it. I stand in awe and find myself incredibly humbled. Paul felt the same.

What was Paul's response?

Humility should always lead us to prayer and praise. To realize our lowly, yet incredibly elevated position is mind-boggling.

In verses 16-19, what are Paul's two main prayer requests?

> **Humility should always lead us to prayer and praise.**

Think about what must be done for Christ to dwell in your hearts through faith and for us to be rooted and grounded in love. What connection is there between "Christ dwelling in our hearts" and "that we be rooted and grounded in love?"

Consider the love God has for us. How well do you (verses 18-19), comprehend the width and length and depth and height of the love of God?

How often do you feel filled with this fullness of God?

On a scale of 1–10 (#1–meaning never feeling the fullness of God and #10–meaning 'always') rate how often through your normal day you feel filled with the fullness of God? _____

Isn't "the fullness of God" an interesting thought? There is a human level where we can sense God's fullness in our everyday. We sense His presence as we go about our schedule when conflict, temptation, and trials arise. His guidance and direction are evident when we intentionally fix our minds on Him. But, there are those moments, that I know far too well, when we are not living in the fullness of God. Those moments when we allow the flesh, self-will, to take control as we judge others, grow impatient, put conditions on our love.

Do you believe that right now you are in a struggle with sensing God's fullness in your life?
In what way(s)?

Has God left you? (Don't believe that lie for a moment. We are always the one that moved.)

As Paul did, praise God that we are included in the mystery and pray to for His fullness today. As for me, I'm going to put on one Princess sock and one red and walk in this mystery all day. My attire might include mismatched socks, but my armor is a perfect fit just for me.

Do you have any prayer concerns today? Be sure to continue using the **Sharpen Your Sword for Week One** and include a sword to use in battle. God is waiting to hear your heart.

Be sure to spend time today memorizing Ephesians 6:10-11.
Write it on the lines below.

_____

_____

_____

The Perfect Fit

Week One   Day Four

Gifts Galore and Clean Underwear

I, therefore, the prisoner of the Lord, beseech you to walk worthy of the calling with which you were called, with all lowliness and gentleness, with longsuffering, bearing with one another in love. Ephesians 4:1-2

As we get closer to our in-depth study of the full armor of God, Ephesians 6:10-18, we'll strive to get the full message of Paul's letter to the Ephesians. Chapter one reminds us that we are rich in Christ with blessings (B) beyond our imaginations. Chapter two tells us it is because we have been made alive (A) in Christ. The mystery (M) has been revealed to us, and we are now, according to Chapter three, fellow heirs in Christ. The foundation has been given.

Have <u>you</u> been made *alive* with Christ?
Were you dead to sin, and now, through faith in Christ and belief in His resurrection, alive?
Do you believe you have rights to the inheritance of Christ?

If so, let's see what we're to do about this position. We have done nothing to gain this gift, except receive it. Once accepted, what do we do? Considering the situation and the undeserved blessings, it should be our deepest passion from a humbled heart of gratitude, to live a life worthy of our high calling, Ephesians 4:1. We should want above all else to live a life glorifying to God. Let's see what Ephesians four has to say.

> **Walk worthy of the calling ...**

Read 4:1-6. List the responsibilities we have to help us walk worthy and glorifying to God.

Chapters one through three give us good footing—a solid foundation. Now, the time has come to walk or live out our faith. The first task we're given is to walk in unity. Isn't it just like God to not only to tell us how to live, best and abundantly, but to give us very practical steps on how to reach that place? To obtain unity in any relationship, these same practical steps must be put in place. Each of us must do our part to be humble, gentle, and patient, bearing with one another in love.

Think of the relational organizations you are part of... marriage, family, workplace, etc. List some areas where you are personally relational with others.

In each of those areas, am I humble, gentle, and patient and set on bearing with one another with love? Do I often want my own way?   Perhaps it was on the phone with a salesman, as a customer at the store, or even in a conversation with my husband. The moment I get on my feet, and on the solid footing of who I am in Christ, Scriptures humble me and I find myself on my knees. I see myself as blessed and yet such a sinner saved by grace. I find myself asking for forgiveness and for grace to live as He desires.

 As we continue to read in verse 4:7-10 what is given to us and to what measure?

What two gifts mentioned do we now possess? Found in Ephesians 2:8 and 4:7.

We have two gifts from a Mighty God, wrapped especially for us. Here is our "G"–Gifts. Can you see them adorned in shiny paper with a tag that says "To _____ (your name), from God?" Have you opened your gifts yet?

When my husband and I were dating and talking about marriage, he surprised me on one Valentine's Day with a small beautifully wrapped gift. Honestly, call me dense, but I had no idea what was in it. All I knew was that the wrapping was exquisite. I raved so much about who wrapped it and how intricate and lovely the outside was that he finally said exasperatedly, "Just open it, will you?" I was so caught up with the wrappings that I almost missed the gift inside. The giver, in this case, my husband, was most excited (and a tad nervous) about the contents–not the way it appeared. In a similar manner, our Giver, God, is concerned that we open the gifts, say, "Yes!" and respond in action.

Read 4:11-16 looking for more gifts.

He didn't leave us alone to work out this *unity* thing, but equipped us with everything we need. He gifted some of his chosen to be: a_____, p_____, e_____, p_____ and t_____.
What are your gifts from God for His glory?

Spiritual gifts are given to the body, the church, as a whole, even though we have received them as individuals. All abilities have come from the hand of God. We are to use them to build HIS BODY with humility, gentleness and patience—and all to God's glory. We are to stay under good teaching by gifted leaders that we may grow. The spiritual gifts of others actually become gifts to us. Through them, we are blessed; our character and lives are enhanced.

Read Ephesians 4:13-16

"Grow Up!" is not a term that usually carries with it positive connotations. Usually, we think it or say it about someone acting in an immature manner. But, oh, how I want to grow up in Christ. I would love to "no longer be as children" (v. 14), but to "speak truth in love" (v. 15), and "grow up in all things into Him." It is knowing who we are (chapters one to three), behaving in that knowledge (chapters four to six), and walking confidently because of Christ. As we grow up physically, we grow out of old clothes. As we grow spiritually, we grow into the full armor.

Read Ephesians 4:17-32. According to this passage, what are some articles of our *old* outfit?

The full armor of God is an outfit chosen for you. It is quite becoming. It flatters you, and it definitely brings out the color of your eyes. It makes you glow! You want to put it on, but first, you must take off the *old outfit* – the dirty undergarments. We've just described these *old clothes* in Ephesians 4:17-32. Let's look at some unflattering, ill-fitting, discolored articles of 4:25-30. List the sin and after it name the correct behavior. (The first one is done for you.)

<u>Lying</u>   – <u>Speaking the truth</u>   _____ – _____

_____ – _____   _____ – _____

According to Ephesians 4:31, what five pieces of clothing must be removed?
1. _____ , 2. _____ , 3. _____ , 4. _____ , 5. _____ .

What three articles of clean clothing do we wear in their place according to Ephesians 4:32? 1. _____ , 2. _____ , 3. _____
Why? _____

 I confess there have been moments in my life when I have struggled with the forgiveness of another. That person hurt me, and I have every right to hold a grudge, protect myself and not forgive. Right? After all, they were wrong. I was innocent. I am better than them!! OUCH! See how quickly that hurt turned to pride? It is time for me to change my attire. Being unforgiving is never attractive. When I pray, the Holy Spirit gently reminds me of how much I have been forgiven. "Who do you think you are, Mona?" Sometimes our *favorite* sin is like that. We wear it, even proudly. We know it's wrong, and it surely doesn't *look good* on us, but we choose to wear it anyway. We justify this hideous-looking attire for the sake of comfort. Can you imagine being comfortable in sin? We excuse ourselves because we have a right to be hateful, or we can't help ourselves. We even blame our heritage. Just yesterday I heard someone say that their red hair was to blame for their short temper! Can you believe it?

Recall a time when you blamed someone else for your bad attitude.

Discard those old garments! Don't even give them to Goodwill or the Salvation Army, just get rid of them. A new clean outfit is needed—a beautiful, designer-fit full armor of God.

Yes, we've been given gifts galore, but they cannot be fully appreciated and effectively appropriated in God's power, unless we are clean. Call me crazy, but I think of these clean clothes as clean underwear for under our full armor of God. And, we all know how important clean undergarments are! (Just ask your mother.)

Perhaps your prayer requests for the day would be to ask forgiveness for some ugly under garments you have been wearing. Include it in **Sharpen Your Sword for Week Two**. Don't forget the verse to stand on.

Continue to write and memorize Ephesians 5:10-11. Let's add verse eleven for this week. You are doing great! Be ready to quote Ephesians 5:10-11 with your study group.

The Perfect Fit

Week One   Day Five

Closet Cleaning

For you were once in darkness, but now you are light in the Lord. Walk as children of light, (for the fruit of the Spirit is in all goodness, righteousness, and truth), Finding out what is acceptable to the Lord. Ephesians 5:8-10

One of my least favorite jobs as mom is cleaning out closets and sorting old clothes. Ugh! Every piece of clothing needs to be touched, examined, sized, tried on and then a decision is made. "Do we keep it?" Two of my three daughters are old enough to do this on their own now. My youngest still isn't certain nor willing to sort for herself. Realizing how quickly they grow, I'm trying to enjoy this dependence as long as I can. I am thankful for the clothes, our home and child… it's just that this chore is not one of my favorites. *Lord, give me the strength to clean our closets with a happy heart.* All you moms know what I'm talking about.

As we go on to chapter five of Ephesians, the sorting of *clothes* continues. It's obvious a new wardrobe is needed. Put it on, so we can *walk in it*, live in it, maybe even, dance in it.

Read Ephesians 5:1-7.

 After we're dressed, according to verse two, what is the most important thing we walk in? Verse four speaks of us walking in _____.

A friend of mine told me when she placed her faith in Christ, the Holy Spirit convicted her of some music and movies she had in her personal collection. She cleaned her closets and discarded all inappropriate items.

As we sort our clothes closet, what are some of the inappropriate pieces of clothing we've been wearing according to Ephesians 5:3-4?

> **Items that are not *fitting*, never compliment.**

STOP. Time for The Pause. Pause, pray and ask the Spirit of God to convict you if any of these are still hanging in your closet and especially if you find yourself wearing them occasionally. Write what He brought to mind.

I love verse three–these articles are not "fitting for the saints." Do we really desire to wear something that is not *fitting* for us? Items that are not *fitting* never compliment.

More inappropriate, unfitting and down-right ugly clothes are mentioned in Ephesians 5:4-7. List them:

The entire filthy line of clothing, mentioned in verses three to six, have a way of getting in my closet and often on my back. Think on these and see if you can relate.

Fornication (sexual immorality)   Uncleanness (any kind of impurity)

Covetousness (greed)   Filthiness (obscenity)

Foolish talk (gossip, boasting)   Coarse jesting (joking, sarcasm)

 Can you think of an example in your life where each of these may pop up? (Hint: entertainment, desiring what another has, gossip, etc.)

My bedroom closet is very dark and I would appreciate a bright light so I could see its contents. In our spiritual lives God sheds His perfect light on our deeds. When we are attentive to His will, we clearly see them. We can see ourselves with purified eyes, we just need to ask.

Read Ephesians 5:8-14. When we walk in His light we make good choices and what do we put on (v. 9)?

Wake up (v. 14), get dressed and realize what time it is (v. 15). God daily gives you opportunity to shine His Light. Get dressed NOW!

Read Ephesians 5:17-21

Most of my music collection is what I call *cleaning music*. When it's time to clean the entire house, a room or just a closet, I choose some upbeat Christian music so I can worship while I work. It keeps me positive and task-centered. (It also helps me to stay grumble-free if it's the fourth time I've cleaned off the table since lunch.) I will hear a good upbeat song and think, "Hmmm, that's great cleaning music." Or I will find a slow, worshipful recording and think, "Oh, that's good cleaning music."

I even enjoy classical music as I clean. Problem was I began realizing that all of my music had become cleaning music. (Sad commentary on time spent cleaning; yet how cluttered the house remained!) As I was reading the musical passage of Ephesians 5:19-21 I realized God created *deep cleaning music* long before I did. As we learn to walk in the Spirit and dress accordingly, we are to "speak to one another in psalms, hymns and spiritual songs, singing and making melody in our hearts to the Lord." God-centered music causes us to give thanks in everything. It changes our outlook and even our attire (from the inside out). Proper behavior (attire) and our actions, filled with music (Spirit-led living) create a cleanliness in us... a cleansing.

Name a favorite recording that you own. Choose a song that sets your mind on God.
What is it? _____. Plan on listening to it today, and *speak it* to another.

As we wrap up Ephesians 5, we realize a few changes may need to be made in our behavior. But, just so we don't get self-confident, Paul brings up a few tricky relationships to spur our thinking. Once our relationship with God is pure because of our repentance and His glorious forgiveness, vertically we are right with God. Up and down, Heaven to Earth, God's heart to mine is good. So what does the apostle Paul do now? He has us look horizontally – our relationships with others. If there is a problem horizontally with a brother or sister it will interfere with the clarity of the spiritual cleaning music. This relational sin will be like static on the radio. We can hear the music but there is an annoying interference, something that is disrupting the pure music we desire to hear. Who knows our strengths and weaknesses better than those that live with us? Ephesians 5:22-33 recalls our actions and reactions in our marriage.

Read the passage and write verse twenty three.

The definition of *voluntary surrender* for submission has always triggered my heart to obey. I could choose to fight God's Word and deal with the consequences of my personal disobedience, or I could voluntarily surrender on my own accord. I know, with my obedience, comes the Lord's blessing.

Read Ephesians 6:1-9. What are the other two personal relationships mentioned in this passage?

Personally, I know I need to check my attire during my parent-child relationships. Is there a part of your parent-child, sibling or daughter-parent relationship that is not honoring to God? How about the master-servant relationship mentioned? Relating that to your workplace or church relationships, is there a horizontal relationship with someone that needs to be surrendered to God? You know, it's that person that just came to your mind. Pray about what God desires for you. When you are in spiritual tune, horizontally as well as vertically, it's like finding perfect clarity on the radio. It's not just sorting and tossing ill-fitting clothes, it's deep cleaning the closet. It's wiping down the walls, vacuuming the floor and shining every shoe. You'll find room to fit new clothes that might include a shield of faith, breastplate of righteousness, shoes of peace, helmet of salvation and sword of the Spirit. You clean yours. I'll clean mine. We'll be ready to put on the full armor of God. Oh, I can hear the music playing already.

 Continue to add concerns, worries and cares to the **Sharpen Your Sword for Week One**.

 You should be reviewing Ephesians 6:10-11 and ready to recite it from memory. Try to write it on the lines. Don't peek. I'll help you out.

"Ephesians 6:10-11.

(10) Finally, be strong _____ and in _____. (11) Put on _____ _____ of God, that _____ against _____.
Ephesians 6:10-11."

The Perfect Fit

Sharpen Your Sword

Week One

Concern	Truth to Believe	Date	Answer
A worry	Proverbs 3:5-6 "He will direct my paths."		

The Perfect Fit

Week One Wrap Up

Principal Questions for Week One

1. List some of the blessings mentioned Ephesians 1:1-14.

2. What are we alive to and how did this take place? (1 Peter 3:18)

3. What mystery is revealed in Ephesians 3:6?

4. According to Ephesians 4:7-10, what is given to us and to what measure?

5. What is the most important thing we walk in after we've dresswed according to Ephesians 5:2?

Practical Questions for Week One

1. List three spiritual blessings that you are certain of in your personal life.

2. Explain what it means to you to be "alive with Christ?"

3. How did you feel when you were included in someone's will?

4. Recall a time when have you blamed someone else for you bad attitude?

5. Can you think of an example in your life where the filthy clothes listed in Ephesians 5: 3-6 may pop up?

The Perfect Fit

Session Two – Reality

[10] Finally, my brethren, be strong in the Lord and in the power of His might. [11] Put on the whole armor of God, that you may be able to stand _against the wiles_ of the devil. [12] For we do not wrestle _against flesh and blood, but against principalities, against powers, against the rulers_ of the darkness of this age, _against spiritual hosts of wickedness_ in the heavenly _places._ [13] Therefore take up the whole armor of God, that you may be able to withstand in the evil day, and having done all, to stand.
Ephesians 6:10-13

The Christian life is a _____, not a playground.

We must know our _____.

  I Peter 5:8   John 10:10   John 16:33b   I John 5:4-5

* He is not a _____ or _____ *He is _____.

Three reasons we are defeated.

We don't know our _____

Unable to _____ ourselves.

Reluctance to go on the _____

_We are doing battle with an enemy who has already _____._

The Perfect Fit

Week Two   Day One

Finally!

"Finally, my brethren, be strong in the Lord and in the power of His might."
Ephesians 6:10

Finally. It seems odd to begin our second week with the word *finally*, knowing that we have seven more weeks to go. Keep in mind that we are at the end of Paul's letter to the Ephesians. *Finally* literally means *as to the remaining* but in this context it means *now to get down to the final plans for attack.* Paul wants Christians to go on the offensive against the unseen forces of Satan. We know we are beyond blessed and have gifts galore, including salvation, but the enemy of our soul does not want us to live victoriously. We do possess all we need for abundant life, yet the enemy desires for us to live defeated lives where we continuously struggle with the same sin. Over and over and over again we fail. That is why we need a change in our attire … *finally*.

We have sped through chapters one to five, to come to a sudden halt at 6:10-20. We were reminded that some items in our attire needed to be removed. And now, (drum roll, please) may I have the honor of opening another gift before your eyes … the full armor of God. (And the crowd goes wild.) I promise you will love the color, style, fit and feel.

Read Ephesians 6:10. What do you think it means to *be strong*?

Ladies, as women we are naturally strong. I understand that we are considered *the weaker sex*, but let's consider childbirth. No weak person can go through labor – especially more than once. The strength of our love for another far outweighs our physical limitations. We overcome. We choose life and love. We are strong.

We must be strong emotionally. We are often strong for our children or our husbands when they are struggling; we become the rock they need. And, what about a weaker sister? We seem to hold the world together. We make time to listen, care and just be there for everyone.

Choose one—Are you a: "Strong Woman"   "Woman of Strength"
                          "Strong Woman in the Lord"   "Strong-willed Woman"

To be "strong in the Lord" states that you are fully aware of where your strength comes. I often find myself in the midst of a trial and get frustrated. I feel helpless, hopeless, or just weary. Perhaps you are in a similar situation right now. It is when I am at that weak place that the Holy Spirit whispers the reminder in my ear that I am possibly responding and reacting in *my own strength*. Yes, I am a *strong woman*, but not *strong in the Lord*. That explains my weakness. I must pause and ask myself if I've prayed and surrendered this to the Father. Or am I *spinning my own wheels* and obviously not sensing God at work in my life? Ever been there?

 Can you recall a time when you were strong in your own eyes?

Was there a point when you were gently reminded, perhaps strongly convicted, that you needed to rest in God? _____ How did you know?

It need not be a life-changing event or trial, but simply a frustrating moment, when looking back you realized you had not consulted God concerning the issue.

I think of Proverbs 3:5-6:

Trust in the Lord with all your heart, and lean not on your own understanding;
In all your ways acknowledge Him, and He shall direct your paths.

At that point I know that I have "leaned on my own understanding." How ridiculous I feel when I realize that I have used my simple, flawed strength, when I have access to "the power of His might."

 Take a moment and examine that power. After each verse describe an attribute of God's power and how it affects us.

Colossians 1:10-12 _____

Psalm 62:11-12 _____

Acts 1:8 _____

2 Timothy 1:7 _____

We are talking POWER! This is the same power that raised Jesus from the dead. Can we begin to grab a hold of this kind of power? Hardly. The same power resides in us. Amazing.

Are you a Strong Woman Or Strong Woman in the Lord?

Do you have a struggle, temptation or trial that you are experiencing? Does it need more power than the power of God?
(Yes, that is a trick question. There is nothing more powerful than God's power.)

We often put limitations on what God can do. We look at the problem through our own eyes, instead of through the eyes of God. We trip over trials when we have been given the power to dance over them. Isn't it about time to *finally* admit that and do something about it?

That is why we need the full armor of God daily. Finally.
Read the following verses and write what we are now *finally* to do.

2 Corinthians 13:11 _____

Philippians 3:1 _____

I Thessalonians 4:1 _____

I Peter 3:8 _____

Wouldn't you love to *finally* be able to "become complete", "rejoice in the Lord", "think on pure things", "abound more and more", and "be of one mind?"

Again, it's all ours when we are "strong in the Lord and in the power of His might."

Think of some routine activities. I'm talking about the daily activities, like doing the laundry, dealing with a difficult person at work, cooking dinner, waking up the family, being alone. Write down two everyday things that you need the power of God to do.

I challenge you to pray about those two situations right now. *"Father, help me to be strong in Your power the next time I ... _____."*

Record it in **Sharpen Your Sword for Week Two**. Include Ephesians 6:10. Let's *finally* do something about it and walk "in the power of His might."

 Begin adding Ephesians 6:12 to your passage of Ephesians 6:10-11. Write it below

The Perfect Fit

Week Two   Day Two

Get Dressed!

"Put on the full armor of God"
Ephesians 6:11a

A one-size-fits-all bright yellow plastic poncho is not flattering for anyone. How can it be? Recently my two oldest daughters, 15 and 17, went to an amusement park with a family from our church. Because of the rain and wind the decision was made that all eight of them were wearing ponchos to attempt to stay dry.

My oldest swore to herself, on an earlier occasion, that she would never wear a poncho. She couldn't imagine ever being desperate enough to wear one. I mean… c'mon. She resisted at first, politely declined and settled on being wet to the bone. The mom of the family finally asked again, "Please, put on the poncho." She agreed, wore the poncho and stayed warm and dry. (Later, she confirmed to me that she wore it only because it was clear. If it had been bright yellow, she wasn't sure what she would have done.)

Paul, being inspired by the Holy Spirit implores us to "put on the full armor of God." Perhaps we're reluctant because we're not sure how we will look in it. I mean, how comfortable can a suit of armor be? But like the poncho, it's for our best.

We find ourselves at a place of decision. We are told to put it on because it is obviously for our best. Shouldn't we desire to wear it? Our Father God prepares it for us, but it is up to us to put it on. We must simply obey. No questions asked. Just put it on piece by piece by piece.

I've asked myself many times "Why?" Why do we struggle to put on the full armor of God when we know it is for our best? Why do we resist putting on the very uniform designed to protect us? Why do we choose defeated lives where we fight spiritual battles with no protection? My final answer— we're sinners. And, lazy sinners at that!

It takes discipline to DAILY put on the full armor of God. To daily surrender our lives to the Creator of the Universe and make Him the Lover of our souls. To daily, shall I say moment by moment, entrust our situations to Him and His control. To spend time in His Word and in prayer means putting on the full armor. Only in His presence is the armor available for our taking. Wearing the full armor shows discipline and decision. It is a sad soldier that obtains a uniform and yet never wears it to live victoriously.

 In the last chapter, we looked at Ephesians 4:22, 25, 31, what were we told to put off? And then in Ephesians 4:24, 32 to put on?

> **Only in His presence is the armor available for our taking.**

Paul tells us to put on truth, good thinking, kindness, new self, righteousness and holiness. These are the same themes he uses in the Ephesians 6 passage of the full armor of God. He is just using a different example to get his point across. Only when an educator has a very important point does he/she take several different avenues to teach the same information, emphasizing its importance.

Let's look in Leviticus 6:8-13 at the Law of the Burnt Offering. Who did God have Moses speak to?

What were their professions? (Jobs in the Kingdom of God)
(Keep a bookmark in Leviticus, we're coming back.)

How does this compare to 1 Peter 2:4-10?

What does that make us? Why?

As believers, free from the Old Testament law, we often read through those passages and do not find the personal application to our spiritual lives. Considering the fact that we are also priests, let's look again at Leviticus 6:8-13 and personalize it!!

According to Leviticus 6:20, what were the priests commanded to put on?
In verse 11, he's told to take off _____ , and then put on _____.
(And you thought your teenager went through lots of clothes.)

The priests were to put on certain garments for specific spiritual jobs God had for them. Whether he was taking the ashes off the altar or carrying the ashes outside the camp, his attire mattered to God. It was for the purpose of purification, but also obedience to the details of God. And, in obedience we must "put on the full armor." (Isn't it beautiful that the full armor takes no laundering, just a decision.)

Again, Moses is commanded to dress someone. The Tabernacle was erected and arranged and God had some specifications for His glory to be present.

Read Exodus 40:12-16.

What was to be *put on* Aaron and his sons? Once they were dressed, what was to be done to them? (v. 15)

Do you believe their anointing as priests correlated with what happens a few verses later in Exodus 40:34-38? What did the 'cloud' symbolize?

> **When we put on the armor, our children and their children benefit.**

Notice the progression.

#1–In obedience they *put on* the specified garments.

#2–Once dressed, the anointing of God was upon them AND THEIR GENERATIONS.

#3–The glory of the Lord filled the tabernacle.

Obedience to get dressed, leads to the anointing by God and His presence overflowing.

This blessing is not only for us, but also for our generations. When we *put on* the armor, our children and their children benefit. Can you think of a better benefit than that? We're not only protected from the elements, like with the poncho, but also blessed in the *putting on*.

May you make the choice DAILY to walk in obedience and put on the full armor as commanded by God. Be ready to be amazed as the glory of the Lord fills your life.

 Complete Sharpen Your Sword for Week Two by writing items on your heart, with promises.

 Continue to review Ephesians 6:10-12.

Let me see if I can help.

Hint #1–Read this repeatedly. Cross out a couple words each read-through. Continue reading and rereading until most words have been omitted.

Hint #2 – Make note that the word "against" is repeated six times. In order, "against the … w", "against the f & b", "against p————-", "against p-", "against the r —-", "against the s h o w".

[10] Finally, my brethren, be strong in the Lord
and in the power of His might.
[11] Put on the whole armor of God, that you may be able to stand
against the wiles of the devil.
[12] For we do not wrestle
against flesh and blood,
but against principalities,
against powers,
against the rulers of the darkness
of this age,
[13] *against spiritual hosts of wickedness*
in the heavenly *places.*

The Perfect Fit

Week Two   Day Three

Why can't I stay in my PJs all day?

... So that you will be able to stand against the wiles of the devil. Ephesians 6:11b

I know on certain mornings I don't want to get up, get dressed and get on with my day. I'd much prefer to stay in my pajamas, robe and slippers and not face the world. In the physical realm, this is okay once in a while, to just veg–out, but in the spiritual realm,–a PJ Day can be quite dangerous. Our enemy will take advantage when our guard is down.

This second part of 6:11 explains why we need to put on our clothes, poncho, I mean, full armor. The storm <u>is</u> coming. The rain <u>will</u> hit hard. The winds will <u>attempt</u> to knock you off your feet...and possibly may. These "wiles of the devil" are inevitable. Be prepared when they come by being dressed in the whole armor of God. The Word does not say, "in case the wiles come your way", it is understood that they will.

When we choose to be armed and ready we choose victory. We must always remember that Satan has already been completely defeated, because of the work of Christ on the cross.

Let's refresh our minds of this glorious fact:
According to Psalm 118:8-14, in whom do we trust and why?

I love the confidence in the Psalmist's voice in verses 13 and 14.

 How might this confidence compare to the statement in Ephesians 6:11?

1 John 3:8 is a difficult passage to understand, but very clear on why the Son of God was manifested.

Why was He?

How does that statement personally apply to you as a Child of God?

The victory is ours through Christ. Satan has been defeated. And, the victory is ours.

It is our position to stand in that truth. Knowing all that to be true, Paul still tells us to be dressed for battle because the enemy is preparing for attack. It is inevitable. The enemy will attack, but we must stand ready knowing full well that the war has been won in Christ and it is in HIS POWER that we can stand at all. What kind of attack does the enemy plan?

What are the "wiles" as mentioned in Ephesians 6:11?

In military terms, the word *wiles* means *stratagems* or battle plans. Satan has detailed plans of attack with perfect execution for our failure. He knows the right timing for these attacks to take place. Satan is not omniscient (does not know everything), omnipotent (does not have all the power), or omnipresent (not present everywhere at one time). Rather, he is incredibly organized!

Remember, he is already perfectly defeated because of the death, burial and resurrection of the Lord Jesus Christ. His wiles continue and we believe the lies he sends our way. We believe them, think on them and then act on them. His wiles come our way (usually in a whisper or a thought) and we begin to stumble instead of stand. Realize, Sister, as believers, Satan cannot stand in our lives unless we give him the place to stand. Oh, how often we do give him that place to stand then he sneakily pushes us, trips us, and watches us stumble.

> **Satan cannot stand in our lives,**
>
> **unless we give him the place to stand.**

We are Satan's target. He knows our weakest places. It is not because he sees into our hearts, but rather because he sees our actions. He knows our failures, because they are evident to all. He's not going to tempt me to rob a bank, that's not a weakness for me. But he does know my tenderness to specific past hurts and chooses to bring them back to my mind again and again. Then I begin the wrestling with emotions and temptations to judge. AHHH!! I need to always remember... I am a target... with a VICTORY sign written in neon lights.

As believers we need *a well thought-out planned counterattack* to put into operation the moment the devil makes a move or else we will fall, unable to STAND as Ephesians 6:11 commands. This counterattack is the armor that God has custom-designed for us and explained in detail in Ephesians 6:10-18.

What does Philippians 1:9-10 explain as the reason that our love must abound more and more in knowledge and depth of insight?

When fully dressed in the armor of God, we are better able to discern what God's will is and what it is not. We are wiser and able to determine God's purposes. God does have a magnificent call on our lives and the enemy does not want it to be fulfilled. Satan fights the hardest when he knows God has something beautiful in store for us. We can discern what the enemy's lie is and what Truth is. We can, using God's defensive and offensive weapons, be prepared and remain battle-ready.

Keep on the look-out! Let's examine 1 Peter 5:8-10.

Verse 8–Who is seeking us?
How is he hunting?

What is his countenance?

What is his goal?

Still in verse 8–Are we surprised by his coming?

Should we be?

After dissecting verse 8, read 9.
What is to be your response?

What are you to do, be and know?

> **Satan fights the hardest, when he knows God has something beautiful in store for us.**

This serves as a reminder that we have a part in the battle. We must put on the armor provided and use it. The warning occurred in verse 8, our response in verse 9 and now, the blessed promise. What is promised to us according to verse 10? "the God of all grace will _____, _____, _____ and settle you."

Don't overlook one key phrase in verse 9. WHEN is the promise provided?

Our God of all grace will be with us to perfect, establish and strengthen us AFTER we have suffered a while. God allows it. God is fully aware and not only gives us what we need to stand, but to be perfected, established and strengthened. It is then that God gets the glory and Satan is again reminded of his defeat.

Be defensive to stand against the wiles of the devil... get dressed piece by piece by piece. Don't stay in your spiritual pajamas. A refining of your character, a strengthening of yourself and an awareness of a personal God will occur. It is promised.

 Be sure to write verses and prayer requests on the **Sharpen your Sword for Week Two** page at the end of this section.

 Add Ephesians 6:13 to the passage memorization of Ephesians 6:10-12. It's the hardest part of all the memory work, but keep on keeping on. God desires you to sharpen this sword. Write Ephesians 6:13.

The Perfect Fit

Week Two   Day Four

Discussion in the Heavenlies

"For we do not wrestle against flesh and blood, but against principalities against powers, against the rulers of the darkness of this age, against spiritual hosts of wickedness in the heavenly places." Ephesians 6:12

I am looking for my glasses. I was called away unexpectedly and when I returned, my glasses were missing. Hmmm… I have no idea. I have retraced my steps with no success. I can survive without them but not as effectively. They are most helpful when reading and definitely bring things into focus for me. (And yes, I have checked the top of my head.)

Paul allows us to see through spiritual glasses into the spiritual realm. He brings all into focus for us. Through his explanation we are able to see the unseen world and the warfare taking place. We know the enemy is real, but how does that affect us personally? We know Christ conquered the wiles of the devil when He resurrected from the dead in all His glory and power. But if you are anything like me, you want to see it for yourself.

We must make Psalm 119:18 our prayer:

"Open my eyes, that I may behold wondrous things out of Your Law."

Open our eyes. If our eyes could be opened to the invisible world, we would be terrified and amazed at the nature of the spiritual activity going on all around us in the heavenlies. There are invisible and unseen rulers who are behind the turmoil and conflict we see. They are Satan and his fallen evil angels. They are not omniscient, omnipotent or omnipresent, but they are organized in ranks.

In our humanness we see struggles, tribulation and trials in the flesh with all their discomfort. But in reality, we do not wrestle with flesh and blood; rather, against spiritual wickedness in high places. We wrestle

> **Our enemy is spiritual, so must our power be.**

with these schemes and wiles that the devil devises to destroy our testimony, faith, and character. At times they seem impossible, it is at that moment we must remember to use the armor God has provided. Our enemy is spiritual, so must our power be.

In addition to this detailed verse of Ephesians 6:12, I Peter 5:8 gives insight into Satan and his schemes. There is the obvious choice in 1 Peter 5:8 (in which we have already looked).

What does it state?

Much is seen of the invisible realm in Job 1:6-12. Understand, Job was a righteous man. In Job 1:6 who came to present themselves before the Lord?

Are you surprised by that?

 In verse 7 the Lord inquired of Satan, "Where have you come from?"

What was Satan's response in the same verse?

What similarities do you find between 1 Peter 5:8 and Job 1:7?

His purpose is not stated in Job, but clearly in 1 Peter. What is Satan's purpose?

Nothing has changed over the years. Satan still seeks to destroy us. He is armed with various stratagems—such as discouragement, frustration, confusion, division, moral failure, guilt and doctrinal error. Satan is still very real and active on the earth. This should serve as motivation to stay close to the Lord.

God puts Job's name out there. Amazing. Why do you think God mentions Job to Satan? Which of these options might it be?

* because God was proud of Job   * to rub Satan's nose in Job's righteousness
* to allow Satan to test him   * other:

I'm not sure why God mentioned Job's name, but I do know when trials come my way, and I surrender them fully to God's power, I grow spiritually. I believe this is part of God's reasoning. Wouldn't you love for God to have such confidence to say of you, "She is blameless and upright, a woman who fears God and shuns evil."

 The dialogue continues in Job 1:9-11. What is Satan's response to God's offer of Job?

Job was blessed and protected by God. We have that same protection when wearing the full armor of God. Hence, another great reason to put it on.

In verse 12 who is given permission? With what restriction?

The account of Job is important to help us understand fully the boundaries under which Satan does his work.

#1 – Satan is accountable to God. All angelic beings, good and bad, are compelled to present themselves before God. (v. 6)

#2 – God knew that Satan was intent on attacking Job. Satan is not omnipresent. His demons work with him, but he is limited. (v. 6-7)

#3 – Satan cannot see into our mind or predict the future, otherwise he would have known that Job would not break under his planned pressure. (v. 9-11) He is not omniscient.

#4 – Satan can do nothing without God's permission. (v. 12)

#5 – Satan can do only what he is permitted. God puts limitations on what Satan can do. Satan is not omnipotent.

Following this meeting with Satan, Job's first test began. What an unimaginable whirlwind. Job's children, sheep, servants, camels, were all destroyed. Read Job 1:13-19.

What was Job's response according to Job 1:20-22?
In one word, what did Job do according to Job 1:20b?

Amazing!

Again a dialogue in the heavens occurs in Job 2:1-7. How did this differ from the first?

Few of us can state that we have ever been through a whirlwind similar to Job's. Yes, we've had our share of struggles and dilemmas, but Job's story seems unmatched.

A few months ago I found myself in a whirlwind of sorts. Within a four day span it came to my attention that (1) one of my daughters had been hurt deeply by a trusted adult (and I needed to intervene with the possible result of a loss of career), (2) another daughter had a problem that needed long term care, (3) our health insurance was to end and I was the one that needed to find work to supply family coverage, (4) a surprise surgery needed to be done ASAP on a different child (it included several months of recovery care), (5-7) etc. It was a lot… a spiritual whirlwind. I sensed God's leading to go to the book of Job and there I found comfort.

Whirlwind was the word God placed on my heart. The Spirit led me to Job as I prayed for direction and peace. In the book of Job, after many tests and poor counsel, Job asks God many questions. The Lord responds in Chapter 38:1.

According to KJV and NKJV, from what does the Lord answer Job?

Isn't that beautiful? I found such comfort in that. He speaks to us, in the midst of our whirlwind or storms of life. He's right there with us. Holding us. And according to Job 38-41, He is reminding us that He is God and we can trust Him.

What is Job's response in Job 42:2?

During my whirlwind, I found the most comfort in Job chapter one. The fact that God stated Job's name was astounding to me. The *very lips of God formed Job's name* in conversation. I had never thought of God's lips speaking my name before in dialogue with Satan, but felt that perhaps a discussion in the heavenlies had taken place. Not for a moment had I thought that I was upright like Job, but I do know that I am blessed and a target of Satan. I felt God's presence during my whirlwind and was confident of God's protection of me.

Just as my glasses bring things into focus in the physical world, God's Word brings things into focus in the spiritual world. (And yes, I found my glasses in my car's visor.) The Word of God brought into focus the truth of the battle for my life taking place in the invisible spiritual world. God is discussing me and the details of my life. Remarkable.

Are there things occurring in your life currently that may be being discussed in the spiritual heavenlies? Does God have your name on His holy lips? What does it sound like?

Record your current whirlwinds in the **Sharpen Your Sword for Week Two**. Perhaps Job has a verse or two that you could use as encouragement.

Read over Ephesians 6:10-13 two times trying to memorize it as a phrase. You're doing great!

The Perfect Fit

Week Two   Day Five

An "Evil" Day

"Therefore, take unto you the whole armor of God, that you may be able to withstand in the evil day, and having done all, to stand." Ephesians 6:13

Knowing we must be strong in the Lord's strength (v. 10), and that we are to put on the full armor of God, because the wiles of the devil are real (v. 11), we are again reminded to take the whole armor of God so that we can stand (v. 12).

Have you ever had an evil day? What does one consist of? Is it one specific day—like the day when the Antichrist rules on the earth? Unlikely. This passage has and continues to discuss victorious living and commands us to dress for success in the full armor of God. I do not believe it is preparing us for one specific day in history. The evil day is undoubtedly a reference to any time the enemy comes against us like a whirlwind; any moment he comes at us with discouragement, frustration, confusion, division, moral failure, guilt, and doctrinal error. The day is evil because Satan and his cohorts are whispering lies to us, and very evil when we begin to debate the truth and validity of the lies.

Read Ecclesiastes 7:14 and rewrite it in your own words.

 In addition to what we learned from Job 1:5-12, what does this verse tell you about God's part in evil days?

Though we cannot see them, we are surrounded by evil beings. It is true that they cannot indwell a true believer, but they can oppress and harass her. We can be certain that if we are not dressed in the armor of God, we can be easily defeated. The beauty is that God has not left us without power and protection to stand in the evil day. He has provided the full armor of God. Our power is the Holy Spirit that indwells us at salvation.

When the evil day comes and we sense discouragement and weakness, it is then we need to use the armor pieces that we have been provided.

Read Ephesians 6:14-17. What are the five pieces of armor mentioned and briefly what does each one represent?

If we are not dressed in the full armor of God, we are easily defeated.

We must have them on before the evil day or moment arrives. It is often too late to put the armor on after the battle has begun. We stand, stumble or fall based on our preparedness. Are you right now ready for an evil day?

 Let's get practical. When the evil day comes and we have the holiness of God to combat it, what is our choice? Do we STAND, STUMBLE or FALL?

Example #1: You're at church and a fellow sister shares her heart with you about a personal matter. You listen and even pray with her. A few days later you are at a picnic with some church friends. Maybe you are even at a prayer meeting. The fellow sister's name comes up and the thought comes to you to share her story, as a prayer request of course.
Do you STAND, STUMBLE or FALL?

Why are we tempted to share something we have been asked to keep in confidence?

Can you think of a Bible verse (or Sword) that you can use at that very moment to bring the Holy Spirit Power into that moment and defeat the enemy? What is it?

Example #2: You're at work and you know of some dishonesty taking place—perhaps a deception against the boss, stealing from the company or a gossip ring generating some steam. One day at lunch you are asked if you know something about the matter. You know at that moment your testimony is at stake.

Do you STAND, STUMBLE or FALL?
Why?

What is a verse that could be used to combat the enemy at that moment?

Example #3: Someone you care about said something very unkind about you behind your back. She and her friends have been talking about you for a long time, but never had the decency to come and talk with you. You go to her and share your heart, hurt and struggle. She apologizes and you forgive, but you are still very uncomfortable around her.

What do you do? STAND, STUMBLE or FALL?

Why?

Is there a verse that could help defeat the enemy's constant attack on your heart and mind?

Example #4: You are trying to gather your family together to get out the door to an outing. Everyone is not moving at the same fast pace that you are and you are becoming frustrated.

Do you STAND, STUMBLE or FALL?

Why?

Is there a verse that could be brought to your remembrance at this time?

Example #5: You've not been feeling well and your doctor informs you that you possibly have a cancerous tumor. He suggests you go to a specialist about the matter.

Do you STAND, STUMBLE or FALL?

Why?

What verse could be used to defeat the enemy and his attack on you at this moment?

I have used some simple evil situations and others more severe. No matter the degree of difficulty, each is an opportunity for you to use the armor that God has provided. Each example comes with a struggle, a possibility for defeat and/or a blessed victorious moment.

Read 1 John 1:9

According to this verse, even when we STUMBLE or FALL, what does God's grace provide?

Oh, how I rejoice in that grace!!

 Pray about a specific evil situation you find yourself in right now. Think on a particular circumstance that is tempting you to be discouraged, fearful, angry or unfaithful—meaning you are stumbling or perhaps fell. God has called us to STAND. He has provided the armor and power to do it.

God has called us to stand. He has provided the armor and power to do it.

Record the situation that you are tripping up over in **Sharpen Your Sword for Week Two**. Pray and record God's whisper to you on what you can do to STAND in the situation, bringing God all the honor and glory.

Write Ephesians 6:10-13 from memory. _____

_____

_____

_____

_____

_____

_____

_____

The Perfect Fit

Sharpen Your Sword

Week Two

Concern	Truth to Believe	Date	Answer
A worry	Proverbs 3:5-6 "He will direct my paths."		

The Perfect Fit

Week Two Wrap Up

Principal Questions for Week Two

1. Describe an attribute of God's power from each of the following verses:

Colossians 1:10-12 _____

Psalm 62:11-12 _____

Acts 1:8 _____

2 Timothy 1:7 _____

2. What are we told to put off and put on in Ephesians 4:22-32?

3. Explain the reason our love must abound in knowledge and depth of insight from Philippians 1:9-10

4. What is Satan's response to God's offer in Job 1: 9-12?

5. In addition to Job 1:5-12, what does Ecclesiastes 7:14 tell you about God's part in evil days?

Practical Questions for Week Two

1. Has there been a point when you were gently reminded by God that you needed to rest in Him?

2. Thinking about the description of an Old Testament priest, how are you described in 1 Peter 2:4-10?

3. How does your confidence in God (Ephesians 6:11) compare to the psalmist's in Psalm 118:13-14,

4. Satan's 'purpose' is described in 1 Peter 5:8 and Job 1:7; what examples of this have you experienced?

5. According to 1 John 1:9, even when we STUMBLE or FALL, what does God's grace provide?

The Perfect Fit

Session Three –
The Battlefield and the Belt of Truth

Ephesians 6:10-14

The Battlefield

The battlefield is in our _____.

2 Corinthians 10:3-5 *For though we _____ in the _____, we do not war according to the flesh. For the weapons of our warfare are not carnal but _____ in God for pulling down strongholds, casting down arguments and every high thing that exalts itself against the knowledge of God, bringing every _____ into captivity to the obedience of Christ, and being ready to punish all disobedience when your obedience is fulfilled.*

Jesus has given us the task of exercising the _____ which He won for _____.

So what do we do?

D –_____ - Examine Your Heart   I John 1:7-9   Psalm 130:3

R –_____ Is there anyone against whom you hold a grudge? Do you gossip?
   Is there anything in which you have failed to put God first? Do you complain?
   Are you "self-conscious" instead of "Christ-conscious"? Do you have an unteachable spirit?
   Do any of the following, in any way, interfere with your surrender and service to God?
   Ambition? Pleasures? Loved ones? Friendships? Desires for recognition? Money? Your own plans?

E –_____ what you believe. Believe it.   2Timothy 1:12-14

S –_____ Exodus 9:11   Romans 5:2

S –Do not _____ Proverbs 3:23

The Belt of Truth–"Stand, therefore, having your loins girt about with truth." (v 14)

I Peter 1:13   John 8:32   2 Tim 2:15   I Peter 2:12   I Peter 3:15-16
Heb 12:1   Eph 4:25

The Roman Soldier would wear a leather belt with an apron that hung in front of soldier's groin and lower abdomen. It was the first protective piece put on and it was used to tie up the garments so as not to get in the way. This would provide freedom in movement, preparedness for battle, and the ability to run with flexibility.

What is "truth" to you? _____

Satan's primary attack is _____, we desperately need truth.

We must be truthful in the everyday; simply _____. Not condoning anger, worry, etc.

Truth is _____. John 14:6 We must live truth and love truth.

We must be controlled by what _____, not by what we think or feel.

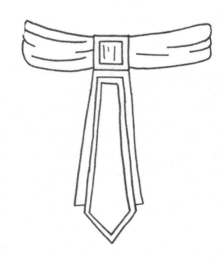

The Perfect Fit

Week Three   Day One

Spiritually Standing

"Stand therefore, having girded your waist with truth…" Ephesians 6:14

Notice the first word in Ephesians 6:13, **Stand**. This is the third time we've been introduced to the concept of standing as part of the requirements of being a soldier for Christ. This idea of *standing* for the Lord was driven home to me several months ago while congregationally singing. The leaders were singing and, as usual, the Spirit whispered in my ear to be on my feet in worship. Out of obedience, I stood. Often, I stand alone and in my heart it is an act of obedience and worship. Many times the enemy whispers in my ear during the worship time. He surely does not want my full focus to be on my Savior in praise. He would prefer I think about myself and what others think of me. When the spiritual wickedness in high places whispers self-thoughts in my ear, I strive not to listen, but admittedly I often wrestle. Because of the past judgments of others, I am at times insecure and concerned of what others think. "What do people think of me when I stand?" "Do I really care?" "Do they think I am trying to be more spiritual than them?" (Heaven forbid that thought, for sure!) The wrestling goes on and on.

I do know it's not all about me. I know I am not really that important to others. *They* do not think that much about me and my actions. But the enemy strives to get my attention onto myself and away from worshipping God for all His goodness. I deliberately turn my attention to the Lord and stand *on the inside* and out. It is a very conscious and deliberate choice. The Spirit whispered to me once, "If you cannot stand for me in the congregation of my children, you will struggle standing out in the world. Practice here." So, I do.

In my church there is an incredibly sweet couple that I love dearly. The lady of the pair enjoys the worship time with much enthusiasm. I love her energy! The gentleman, due to struggles with diabetes, has had one leg amputated and toes removed on the other. As usual, on this particular Sunday morning, I was seated behind them and the worship music was sweet to my heart. The Spirit encouraged me to stand, and I did, but not without some spiritual wrestling. Soon after I was on my feet, the dear lady ahead of me stood to hers. (We were the only two for a while.) Then the gentleman strived to stand to his. He could not. He struggled and even with her assistance, and a little of mine, could not manage to rise on his prosthetics. He gently waved for her to stop helping and remained seated. The praise continued and his struggle to stand was not noticed by anyone. It seemed the struggle was over, but in my heart, God was doing a work.

While everyone was singing praises to our God, I watched several tears flow slowly down the dear gentleman's cheek. He wanted to stand and worship, but physically could not. He wanted to be on his feet, fully surrendered to the God of the universe, but he could not make it happen. God knew his heart and it was clear that he was worshipping with all he had. He was fully surrendered to the Lord. <u>He was standing in his full armor in worship.</u>

> **He was standing in his seat, while I was sitting on my feet.**

The parallels were striking to me. There I was spiritually wrestling, while he was physically wrestling. No one knew of my struggle, but a few knew of his. And yet, *he was standing in his seat, while I was sitting on my feet.* I was humbled and convicted and began discussing with the Lord what it truly means to *stand* for him.

What does it mean to you to *stand* for the Lord? For the base of this study, it means you are dressed in truth, righteousness, peace, faith, salvation and the Word. According to the aforementioned story, it is a full surrender, not concerned for a moment what others may think or say. It is being focused deliberately on the Lord of our lives. No turning back.

In the Greek, *steko* (stay-ko) means to stand. Translated, it means to stand firm, to persevere, to persist, to keep one's standing. We researched the word *stand* last week and then again today. Nowhere in the definition does it have anything to do with being on our feet physically. We can stand spiritually and be seated. I have no disagreement with that.

Read Luke 7:36-50 and answer the following questions.

In the beginning of verse 38 the woman was standing, but how do we know by the end of that same verse she was not?

What actions, portrayed by her, show she was standing spiritually even when physically not?
While worshipping, are the "powers of darkness" whispering things (lies) in her ear?

> **We do need to be on our spiritual feet during our spiritual battles.**

Does she have reason for discouragement?

Is she concerned about what others think?

   What did Jesus say about her spiritual stature?

(Which verse proves it?)

Although we do not need to be on our physical feet during worship, we do need to be on our spiritual feet during the spiritual battles. We must not stumble and stay low, but stand completely convinced that the victory that we have is the Lord's, and He will do what He has promised. We must be prepared, ready and standing when the enemy and his forces begin to feed his lies our way. Spiritually standing and ready for battle is a must.

In closing for today, let's look at 2 Thessalonians 2:13-15.

13But we are bound to give thanks to God always for you, brethren beloved by the Lord, because God from the beginning chose you for salvation through sanctification by the Spirit and belief in the truth, 14to which He called you by our gospel, for the obtaining of the glory of our Lord Jesus Christ. 15Therefore, brethren, stand fast and hold the traditions which you were taught, whether by word or our epistle. 2 Thes 2:13-15

   How does knowing you are brethren beloved by the Lord encourage you to stand firm, persist in your faith, and persevere through difficulties? (v. 13) _____

_____

_____

Look again at verse thirteen. How does knowing that God chose you for salvation through sanctification by the Spirit and belief in the truth compare with the 13th verse of Ephesians 6 when you are commanded to stand therefore with your waist girded in truth? (Think about the gift of God and our part in the process.)

And finally, 2 Thessalonians 2:15 tells us to stand fast and hold the traditions you were taught. How can we practically in spiritual battle, practice these two verbs—stand and hold?

My dear gentleman friend chose to stand. The Sinful Woman of Luke seven, chose to stand. I want to stand fully dressed in the armor.

Knowing you are beloved of the Lord, chosen for salvation, and through sanctification growing every day, name one place or way you can <u>stand</u> in your faith today. Be specific.

 Be sure to add any prayer requests to the **Sharpen Your Sword for Week Three**. Choose a verse for each request from *Swords from the Armory*.

 The memory work this week is a breeze after last week. You only need to add Ephesians 6:14a, "Stand therefore, having girded your waist with truth." Be sure to recite it from the beginning, "Finally, my brethren …" What treasures you are adding to your heart. What training you are doing to your mind.

The Perfect Fit

Week Three   Day Two

Gird Your Waist!

"Stand therefore, having girded your waist with truth…" Ephesians 6:14

Oh, the humor in scripture. How I smile at the irony of the words *waist and truth* in the same verse. Talk about a delicate subject with women. ☺ God cuts right to the personal matters and so shall we today–girding our waist with truth.

We know a belt is to be used to hold up our pants or skirt. It is usually best fitted while in the standing position. A few weeks ago in church a woman of 82 years stood to sing, only to have her skirt fall to her knees. I bet she wished she had had the belt of truth tied around her waist. Although she laughed about it with ease and was grateful for wearing a slip, the actualization of being vulnerable became a reality. Draw a mental picture of yourself waving a sword at Satan with one hand, while you clutch your skirt with the other. Hmmm… rather clumsy and not very effective. We would definitely be unprepared for battle. We need to put on the belt of truth.

There are two different historical interpretations of the belt of truth. The military belt referenced was named after a sturdy leather belt with an apron that hung in front of the Roman soldier's groin and lower abdomen. Paul would have seen the guard wearing this style belt while being held under house arrest. Small brass plates were attached to the apron to provide the greatest possible protection. The jangling noise, made by the apron, when the legionaries marched, helped to intimidate the enemy. These belts are called the *cingulim*. It was the first piece of protective gear worn. Although it was not the most noticeable piece of the armor, it was actually the central piece that held all the rest securely in place, and provide for every need during battle. The belt had specialized holders and hooks on which to secure the scabbard–that contained the sword at the proper angle, the quiver–which held lances, and an apparatus on which to rest the large battle shield. On the belt were clips with which to hold the breastplate in its proper place. Supplies of bread, oil and water were also on the belt.[1]

In Asian countries, during Paul's time, people wore girdles to bind up their flowing garments and hold everything together. Even thousands of years earlier we read of Elijah in 1 Kings 18:46 as he girded up his loins and ran ahead of Ahab. Let's take a moment and look at this inspiring story of Elijah.

Read 1 Kings 17:1 What was the proclamation of Elijah, God's prophet?

In the next chapter, 18:1, what was his proclamation?

Doesn't it sound like a message simple enough to deliver? "No rain." "Rain is coming."
But continue reading 1 Kings 18:1-19 for the acceptance of his prophetic statement.

 Who was Obadiah and how did he respond to seeing Elijah?
(I find such humor in the babblings of Obadiah. Can't you almost hear his desperation?)

The Israelites had drifted so far from God that they were now worshipping the foreign god of Baal. Elijah knew these fallen people needed to be reminded of the true God. Now the chapter continues with a great standoff between Elijah and prophets of Baal. Rain was on the way. God was sending it. And Elijah was God's messenger. He was not a soldier but, at this moment, was fighting some serious spiritual warfare. He had his spiritual belt of truth on, ready to proclaim God's will. What question does he ask the Israelites in I Kings 18:21?

What was their response? _____

_____

_____

_____

 Sad, isn't it?
But if that same question were asked of you, what would your response be?

CHOOSE ONE. That's the only option God gives us. We can't serve two... not well. And definitely not dressed in the armor of God.

In verse I Kings 18:22, Elijah states that he is alone left a prophet of the Lord, in comparison to Baal's 450. The story continues and the competition is on. Elijah's God vs. Baal.

Read 1 Kings 18:23-29. Compare the actions of the prophets of Baal to our actions when we are serving other gods–ourselves, the approval of others, money, etc.

1 Kings 18:30 is a favorite from this passage...

> *And he repaired the altar of the LORD that was broken down.*

The Israelites had wandered so far from worshipping and serving the true God that they had allowed the altar of the LORD to be destroyed. Sometimes we need to re-build our altar. Before we attempt to put on the belt of truth or any piece of the armor of God, we must be cleansed of sin. We must go to the altar of the LORD and pray for a cleansing of His Spirit.

Perhaps you are at a pivotal place of decision. Whom will you serve? God or yourself? _____

Read 1 Kings 18:31-40.
Did the flame consume the sacrifice or the sinner?

Is that a wonderful solution from an unconditionally-loving God?

And to finish the story in verses 41-46, the drought ends for there is **a sound of abundance of rain** (v. 41). Ahab interestingly obeys Elijah's commands. Hmmm, and he's the king. Elijah practices faith in action when God's truth is prevalent. Elijah knew the rain was coming when no one else could see it. He even heard the sound of abundance of rain when there was not a cloud in sight. Even after his servant checked seven times!

> **Is there something you have been praying for and cannot see an answer in sight?**

 Is there something that you have been praying for, working toward, and yet, cannot *see*, or even *hear* an answer in sight? Put on your belt of truth, knowing that God hears his children.

How can wearing our belt of truth improve our faith?
We know the truth of God's Word and we know He is Truth, with a capital "T." He is faithful to His Word. This confidence comes in sporting, with authority, the belt of truth.

> **The sky became black with clouds and wind and there was a heavy rain.** (v. 45)

The blessing came in the form of a storm.
Life is like that sometimes, isn't it?

Then the hand of the LORD came upon Elijah,
and he girded up his loins
and ran ahead of Ahab to the entrance of Jezreel. (v. 46)

> **The blessing came in the form of a storm.**

Elijah was practically gathering his flowing gowns together so he could run in the rain. But isn't that what we do when we gather ourselves together in full surrender to the LORD and gird up our loins? Sometimes it is to run in the rain. When we are in God's strength, we always win the race against the enemy. We are empowered by the Lord God and defeat the enemy.

In closing, let's look at Luke 12:35-37. What is girding one's loins a sign of? _____

_____

_____

When we gird ourselves with the belt of truth it is in readiness for service. ACTION.

Gird yourselves and be ready to stand, and then, walk in truth. Even if that means a run in the rain. The truth is, God is in the rainy storm with us.

Oh, Lord. Help me to choose to stand, and put my belt of truth on, so that I may be ready to run in the paths you have for me. Help me to be so inclined to You, and the truth of Your Word, that no matter how you decide to lead, I will follow... trusting You. I want to defeat the enemy in Your strength. Rebuild my altar, so it is a pure place to worship You in truth.

Write today's prayer request on **Sharpen Your Sword for Week Three**.

Continue to review Ephesians 6:10-14a.

The Perfect Fit

Week Three   Day Three

A Woman of Integrity

"Stand therefore, having girded your waist with truth..." Ephesians 6:14

Okay, I confess, I just told a lie. It was a little one and no one got hurt. In fact, my lie helped to keep peace in the family. Really. If I had told the truth there would have been some sparks flying. So, wasn't I justified in this one little lie?

It's like this—my youngest daughter is spending the night at a friend's house. She just called at 8:30 a.m. to be sure I fed her fish last night and then again this morning. Her direct question to me was, "Mom, did you feed my fish last night?" I responded with an energetic, "Sure, I did, Honey." Truth was, I had completely forgotten. Then, she asked if I did this morning. While on the phone with her, I walked to her room to feed her fish, praying it was still alive and well. Phew, he's still swimming. She was grateful and no one got hurt. (Okay, maybe the fish went to sleep hungry. But do fish even sleep? That's another story.)

No big deal. Right? Wrong. Because I now need to write about being a woman of integrity and the crazy feed-the-fish-lie is on my mind. Give me a minute. I need to repent to the LORD, apologize to my daughter and the fish. I'll be right back.

********* ********* ********* ********* *********

Done. Thanks for your patience. I'm forgiven on every account.

Was I wearing my belt of truth when I answered with a lie? Obviously, not! That, or it wasn't tightened securely enough and my slip was starting to show. Either way, the enemy whispered "convenience—family peace" in my ear and I responded his way. Why? Because I wanted my daughter to know I remembered what was important to her. I wanted to be *Super Mom* yet again. Silly, huh? Not silly to me. It's those day-in and day-out decisions that determine my character. The ways I respond to the enemy's lies determine to whom I am truly listening. It comes down to integrity and honesty.

Aletheia (a-lee-thee-a) is the Greek word for *truth*. It is the reality lying at the basis of an appearance. Aletheia is that which agrees with the final reality. Dependability. Accuracy. Integrity. Veracity. Sincerity. The whole truth. Nothing but the truth.

The word truth, as mentioned in Ephesians 6:14, is the *aletheia* as mentioned in the following passages from Ephesians 4.

Read each and write down what *truth* means practically to us as women in each verse.

Ephesians 4:15 _____

_____

Ephesians 4:21 _____

_____

Ephesians 4:25 _____

_____

Since Paul is the author of the entire book of Ephesians, we could assume that his intent with the *truth* mentioned in chapter four carries the same meaning as that mentioned in the "belt of truth." We must be ready to walk in this truth and wear the belt fully aware of its presence.

1, 2 and 3 John have something to say about this action-packed truth also.

What is truth referred to in the following verses?

1 John 4:6 _____

_____

2 John 4 _____

_____

3 John 4 _____

_____

It is a decision we make to gird ourselves with truth.

Where does that decision take place in reference to 1 Peter 1:13?

> **Never does one accidentally become a Godly woman.**

Do we truly desire to be women of integrity, wearing the belt of truth? I often think of Godly women that have meant a great deal to me over the years. These women that have mentored me through difficult seasons and inspired me to a deeper walk with God. They have worn, and wear, the full armor of God daily, in and out of challenging situations. Some, I've never met; yet, their writings inspire me. The belt of truth has looked entirely different in each life, yet always flattered their entire countenance and enhanced their individual beauty.

One does not wake up one morning a woman of integrity. It takes years of making the truthful decision in every situation. It takes study and practice of God's word. It takes memorizing the word, until it becomes a part of who you are. It takes time and full surrender. It all comes with a determination and decision to wear the armor and be a woman after God's heart. It is intentional. Never does one accidentally become a Godly woman. We choose daily. Oh, how I strive, in God's strength, to be such a woman!

When we go into battle, we better go with integrity, honesty to ourselves, and sincerity. It is possible to go through our Christian lives knowing enough to carry on an intelligent conversation with another equally uninformed believer, but be completely unable to use truth against Satan... making us vulnerable to his attack.[1]

I'm learning, the hard way, that a woman of integrity knows how to practice 1 Peter 3:15 and 16. Look up this passage and write (1) what we are to do and (2) how to accomplish it.

Most of us as women always have something to say. It might be some wisdom to share with our children, an opinion to express to our husband or just a good story that follows the line of conversation. My husband and I have been blessed with three daughters that each have opinions and something to say. I was just sharing with one of them about the wisdom of learning to keep your mouth shut at the right moment. A lesson I am still learning.

According to 1 Peter 3:15 we are encouraged to give an answer to everyone who asks us to give the reason for the hope that we have. Verse sixteen reminds us to do it with gentleness and respect. These are opportunities to live truth, just not speak it. After all, our actions speak louder than our words. Our walk talks louder than our talk talks. My interactions with impatient co-workers, unappreciative family members, or rude cashiers, must be foundationally built on kindness and truth. I try to give them a piece of my heart, rather than a piece of my mind.

There are times when I must speak and then there are times when silence is the best way to practice being a woman of integrity. It seems we learn more when we listen. Everyone wants someone to listen to their heart. Listening teaches me humility of the heart, which goes hand in hand with truth in the heart. Intentionally listening to another shows respect for them and perhaps shows them the love of God that they desperately need to embrace. When I listen more than I speak, I am not as tempted to speak unkind words about another.

> **Our walk talks louder than our talk talks.**

Examine your own heart. Do you listen more than you speak?

Do you agree that it should be a goal of a Godly woman? Why or why not?

Read and respond to the following truths. How are we are to include them in our lives.

1 Samuel 12:24 _____

_____

Psalm 25:5; Psalm 51:6 _____

_____

 The following verses imply that wearing the belt of truth is a choice. What do you think? Psalm 86:11 and Proverbs 8:7

Do you choose to wear the belt of truth by being a woman of integrity?

 Write down any prayer requests that came to your mind today on your **Sharpen Your Sword for Week Three**. Is there a situation where you might not be as truthful as you ought? Choose a verse to correlate.

 Write Ephesians 6:14 on the line below. Be sure to add it to Ephesians 6:10-13.

The Perfect Fit

Week Three   Day Four

God Is Truth

"Stand therefore, having girded your waist with truth..." Ephesians 6:14

*J*ohn 14:6 Jesus said to him, **"I am the way, the truth and the life. No one comes to the Father except through me."**

Jesus is Truth. Jesus is *Aletheia*. He is absolutely pure and righteous. There is no darkness in him at all. He cannot lie. The full armor of God is only for those that have already accepted Christ's death on the cross as payment for their personal sin. Whether we trust Him or not, He is still Christ, the Son of God. He is holy. Our belief or unbelief doesn't change a thing. He is God. Jesus is part of the Godhead with the Father and Holy Spirit. That is Truth–with a capital T.

I have accepted Jesus as my Savior. I believe fully that He is God and Truth in every sense. He is truly the way, the truth, and life; for he is <u>my</u> *way* to salvation, <u>my</u> *truth* for everyday living, and <u>my</u> *life* in heaven and <u>my</u> abundant *life* on earth. It is personal and I love Him.

I sin against a holy God. I am so far from perfect, and yet because of Christ's death on the cross, I am forgiven. I can be daily cleansed and completely pure in the sight of our Almighty God. Below are a few verses from the Holy Word of God. Look up each and write a truth that you believe today.

John 3:16 _____

_____

Romans 3:21 _____

_____

Romans 5:8 _____

_____

Romans 6:23 _____

_____

Deuteronomy 32:4 _____

_____

Psalm 119:160 _____

_____

Jesus is also the Word (John 1:1, Revelation 19:13). This makes the Word of God, Truth as well. Understanding the Word, the Bible, as Truth isn't always easy. To help us gain understanding, Jesus promised a guide—the Holy Spirit.

Write down the truths found in John 14:25.

The Holy Spirit leads us into the Truth and will explain spiritual things as we delve into the Word of God. He will convict us when necessary so that we can be pure vessels He can work through. He will cast light in the shadows of the heart where sins are hidden. He will peel off the masks of deceit that we so often wear thinking no one can see. He will reveal truth to us.

All that I have written above is Truth. It is the understood truth that we wrap around us like a belt. How do I know this? I have accepted it by faith. All of these truths are the threads that make up the belt of truth. When we live it, we sport the belt of truth in a God-honoring way.

We need to remember that the enemy will often try to distort the truth, twist it, and those not entirely filled with the Holy Spirit, or wearing the full armor of God, will be misled. We discussed fully in Week #2, that Satan is the deceiver. His only goal is to destroy us. He cannot take our salvation and eternal life away, but he can surely keep us from enjoying the abundant life that we have been promised. He knows how to confuse us and steal our joy.

Read John 8:31-47 and answer the following questions.
What must we do to be a disciple of Jesus? And what do we receive in exchange? (v. 31-32)

 Why were the Jewish believers confused in verse 32?

> **These truths are the threads that make up the belt of truth.**

What is a slave to sin? And who is their father? (v. 34-38)
From where did Jesus come? (v. 39-42)
Name four facts about the devil from verses 44-47.

A couple years ago I read, Nancy Leigh DeMoss' book, Lies Women Believe. She begins the first chapter with these words: "Jesus came to give us abundant life, but so many of us live defeated, stressed-out, lonely, fearful lives. The problem is that we have believed a lie, one of any number of lies in Satan's arsenal. Oh, we don't have to believe all of his lies; in fact, many of us would probably pride ourselves on not believing many of his lies. But there may be just one, just one little lie hanging like a luscious piece of fruit, one little lie that we have picked and eaten. Not one of Satan's lies is harmless. We need to be able to discern those lies when we hear them, to counter them with the Truth, and to help others do the same."

Following is a list of some of the lies Satan may have whispered in your ear. Place a check beside the one(s) that you have listened to and possibly acted upon. Pray that the Holy Spirit gives you discernment to shed some light on them and to with spiritual eyes see them as the lies they are. We cannot wear the belt of truth while believing lies and living them. We must love truth and live truth if we are to defeat the enemy in our full armor.

"Lie List" Adapted from the chapters in Lies Women Believe

_____ God is not good.

_____ Following God leads to misery.

_____ You are inferior and worthless.

_____ You can't help yourself.

_____ You are not pretty enough.

_____ This sin is no big deal.

_____ You are too busy to have a quiet time with the Lord.

_____ You need a man to be happy.

_____ You have a right to expect others to serve you.

_____ Children must go through a rebellious stage.

_____ You are 100% responsible for our children's actions.

_____ You can't control your feelings.

_____ You can't forgive.

_____ You can't help being moody and mean during your time of the month.

_____ If your circumstances were different, you would be different.

_____ This circumstance will never change.

_____ God can't love you.

_____ God should fix all your problems.

_____ You need to love yourself.

_____ You have a right.

_____ This one time won't hurt.

_____ You can't get victory over 'this' sin.

_____ You should try to change your husband.

_____ "It's all about you."

_____ If you 'feel' it, it must be true.

_____ You have a right to remain angry.

_____ You shouldn't have to suffer.

_____ God made a mistake this time.

I understand this is a very partial list, but it will get you thinking about how often the enemy whispers lies in our ears, we listen and act instead of testing it against the truth of God's Word. In order to gird ourselves with the belt of truth, we must remove the lies from our hearts, lives and minds.

Were you surprised at how many lies you have listened to and believed?

From the Lie List circle a favorite lie or two that you have wrestled. Write it or them below. Why do you think you struggled with calling it a lie?

 After checking the Lie List, reference Psalm 25:5 and Psalm 86:11. From those verses write a prayer of truth. Perhaps you could include it on the **Sharpen Your Sword for Week Three**.

 Fill in the blanks with the correct words from Ephesians 6:10-14.

Finally, my brother, _____His might,

Put on _____devil.

For we do not _____ but,

Against _____, against _____, against _____,

Against _____. Therefore, take up _____
_____ evil day, and _____to stand.

Stand therefore, having _____ with truth.

The Perfect Fit

Week Three   Day Five

"What Is Truth?"

"Stand therefore, having girded your waist with truth…" Ephesians 6:14

We know to spiritually stand, gird ourselves for action, live a life of integrity and not believe the lies of the enemy. Doing all of this we can gird ourselves with the belt of truth, but there is still one question that I find in John 18:38 that is nagging at me relating to truth. During the cross examination of Jesus by Pilate, on the eve of his crucifixion, Jesus states in **John 18:37, "You say *rightly* that I am a king. For this cause I was born, and for this cause I have come into the world, that I should bear witness to the truth. Everyone who is of the truth hears my voice."** Pilate's answer to this statement was, **"What is truth?"** Pilate was searching for it then and the world is searching for it still. What is truth? We believe Truth to be the living God and that life can be found in Him. But daily truth is needed in everyday situations. We can deal with truth. We can put our arms around it. We have a firm foundation on which to begin.

Many years ago a friend confided in me that her husband had been having an affair. He lied to her numerous times and it was no longer possible for her to decipher between the lies and truth. The question, "What is truth?" was voiced by her many times. She told me over and over again, "I can deal with the truth, I just can't stand the lies."

Another dear friend is currently going through tests to determine if she has breast cancer. The doctors continuously tell her information and encourage her to get another opinion. The more opinions she gets, the more she asks, "What is truth?" She just wants to know the truth so she can begin to deal with her health issues.

My child comes home from an activity and tells me the happenings of the evening. I hear through the grapevine a different story. When I confront my child, she re-explains the story with a different slant. I sense a lie growing. I ask, "What is truth?" Let's deal with the facts and get to the root of the issue.

The beauty about God is that He cannot lie. He never lies, not even little white ones. His promises are Truth and we can trust them. They give us a firm foundation that we need to build on. I use the word *beauty* because truth is a beautiful thing. It is flattering in every sense of the word. We may not believe them to be at the moment of truth–like when we stand on a scale, or look in the mirror in the morning–but it is at that moment we can begin to improve, grow, build, and become more like Christ.

Sometimes we realize we have believed a lie, acted on it, and have now found ourselves in a difficult situation. We have repented, but there is still much damage that has been done. We have apologized and asked forgiveness in accordance with God's Word, but things seem like they will never be the same. What do we do? The truth has shed its light and we don't know where to begin.

Gird yourself with the belt of truth. If you have prayed for forgiveness and in obedience did what the Spirit directed you to do, then put on that belt proudly. The blessing will follow. Surround yourself with Godly people that will encourage you and spur you on to grow in Christ and His Word.

 Look up the following verses and complete the sentences.

> **Truth is
> a
> beautiful
> thing.**

John 1:12   I am God's _____.

John 15:15   I am Christ's _____.

1 Corinthians 6:17 I have _____.

Ephesians 2:18   I have _____.

Colossians 1:14   I am _____.

Romans 8:28   I am assured that _____.

Hebrews 4:16   I can find _____to help in my time of need.

If you believe and practice these truths, your belt of truth will fit you perfectly for whatever situation you find yourself in and *you will be real*. Ahh... I love that word... real. It is the passion of my heart to be real, genuine, with a *this-is-who-I-am-all-the-time* authenticity. I deeply desire and strive to be the same Godly woman at 7:30 a.m., when I'm hurriedly getting everyone out the door for school and work, as I am in the midst of worship time in church on Sunday morning. Y'know what I'm talking about. I want my children and husband to see the same Mona that my Sunday school class sees. It is truly the passion of my heart and the truth I strive to wear always.

What does your belt of truth look like?

It surely does not need to resemble the heavy artillery belt of the Roman soldier. Paul was speaking in visuals and allegories, so let's take it one step further and feminize it for ourselves. It is pink? Leather? Tasseled? Fabric? Long and flowing? Made of flowers? Created of ribbons? Describe it.

I'll tell you what mine looks like. It is a long flowing wide gold ribbon, very feminine and beautiful. It is flattering on me and I picture Jesus handing it to me and assisting me in putting it on. Obviously, He is the Truth and without Him I cannot wear it. For without Him I cannot do any good deeds. But with Him—Watch out!—I am ready to be amazed.

"What is Truth?" Jesus and every word He ever spoke. His Spirit is alive in me.

 Pilate searched for it and He, our Lord Jesus, was right in front of him. We may find ourselves searching for truth. Look no further. Just talk to Him in prayer. He's right in front of you. Waiting to hear your heart. Then wear your belt of truth by living a life of integrity glorifying to God. Write in **Sharpen Your Sword for Week Three**.

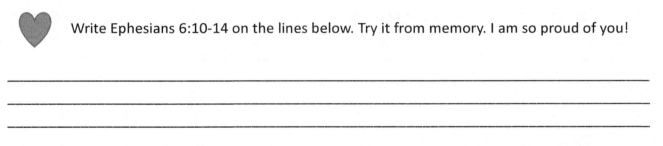 Write Ephesians 6:10-14 on the lines below. Try it from memory. I am so proud of you!

_____

_____

_____

_____

The Perfect Fit

Sharpen Your Sword

Week Three

Concern	Truth to Believe	Date	Answer
A worry	Proverbs 3:5-6 "He will direct my paths."		

The Perfect Fit

Week Three Wrap Up

Principal Questions for Week Three

1. How did Jesus describe a woman's spiritual stature in Luke 7: 36-50?

2. Read 1 Kings 18:1-19; how did Obadiah respond to seeing Elijah?

3. Explain the relevance of truth in

Ephesians 4:15

Ephesians 4:21

Ephesians 4:25

4. According to John 8:34-38, what is a slave to sin? And who is their father?

5. Reinforce these truths:

I am God's _____ (John 1:12)

I am Christ's _____ (John 15:15)

I have _____ (1 Corinthians 6:17)

I have _____ (Ephesians 2:18)

I am _____ (Colossians 1:14)

I am assured that _____ (Romans 8:28)

I can find _____ to help in my time of need. (Hebrews 4:16)

Practical Questions for Week Three

1. How does knowing you are loved by the Lord encourage you to stand firm, persist in your faith, and persevere through difficulties?

2. How would you respond to the question, "How long will you waver between two opinions?"

3. Do you believe the wearing of the belt of truth is a choice? (Psalm 86:11 and Proverbs 8:7)

4. Remembering the 'Lie List' which type of lie do you wrestle with?

5. Using visuals and allegories, what does your belt of truth look like?

The Perfect Fit

Session Four – The Breastplate of Righteousness

Ephesians 6:14b. "… and having on the breastplate of righteousness;"

Is 59:16-17   Titus 3:5   Phil 3:9   Gal 2:20-21   Lev 19:15   Heb 1:9
2 Thes 3:3   Rom 1:17, 3:22

The Roman soldier would wear curved metal bands or chain mail constructed by linking small metal rings together until they formed a vest. It would protect viral organs, and cover the front from neck to upper part of the thighs.

What is "Righteousness" to you? _____

Do we become righteousness – at Salvation? In ourselves or Jesus' righteousness on our account? We are _____ or "declared righteous" through the merit of Jesus. Satan attacks—_____ us of our sin, but cannot take away our _____

Self-righteousness Is 64:6 vs. God's righteousness. Phil 3:8-9
_____ makes us susceptible to Satan's wiles. 2 Cor 2:9-11
_____ Righteousness – "Practical ighteousness" Eph 5:18

Not only standing in the righteousness of Christ, but _____ Him in our conduct in _____ _____ "Spirit Filled" Only when we yield to _____ _____ and obey the Word that our walk changes and reflects righteousness. We stand before God by the righteousness of Jesus Christ, We stand before man in His righteousness produced in us. _____ is the Righteous One. Is 59:16-17

The Perfect Fit

Week Four   Day One

Breastplate of Righteousness

"...having put on the breastplate of righteousness." Ephesians 6:14b

Okay ladies, what immediately comes to *your* mind when you think of a woman's perspective of the breastplate of righteousness? My mind goes to Wonder Woman and that bronze bra-like top she wore as she rescued the world from harm. Remember? I can recall, but not relate. I've heard jokes about being on the small side up on top as long as I can remember. As a teen it bothered me, but now I've accepted God's design for me.

I can almost hear my brothers teasing me when for my 16th birthday, my parents gave me a wooden hope chest as a gift. The idea was that at 16 years old I was to start thinking about the future and marriage and putting things away for that day. And the beautiful wooden hope chest that my Dad chose was to be the perfect item to put them in. As I type, I can look to my left and see it in <u>my</u> home today. It's nearly been thirty years since they brought it home and I can still remember the comments from my brothers. "There's Mona, hoping for a chest. Ha! Ha! Ha!" I smile about it now, because I am confident of their love for me, but 30 years ago, it caused me some hurt.

Honestly, I'm way past hoping for a chest. But hoping for a breastplate of righteousness? Now, that's a goal. And, as a believer, it's already mine. I just need to put it on daily. Please note, although it is provided, it is our place to put it on. This week we'll dig into what that really means.

As Paul was attached to the Roman soldier during his homebound imprisonment, he had the visual before him of the soldier's breastplate. The soldier would have fastened one of three types of breastplates around his chest during that time period. The first was fashioned by joining several broad, curved metal bands together, using leather thongs and called *a lorica segmentata*. The second was a type of chain mail, constructed by linking small metal rings together until they formed a vest. This one was called a *lorica hamata*.[1]

The third type of breastplate is my personal favorite. It was truly a work of art, customized and made for the soldier that wore it. Often a casting was made of the man's torso. This negative casting was then used to make a positive of the torso. The positive casting, the breastplate, was overlaid with brass that was beaten to conform to the details of the torso. Breastplates were often made very elaborate with additional decorations and polished to a brilliant mirror finish that was blinding in the sunshine.[2]

The purpose of each was the same—to protect the soldier's vital organs. Without this breastplate of protection, an arrow could easily reach a soldier's chest, piercing his heart or lungs. Some breastplates covered the front from the neck to the upper part of the thighs. All were very functional and extremely strong, yet created a flexible defense against enemy swords and stabbing weapons. They provided safety and convenience.

Turn to Exodus 39:1-30. In this account of the making of the priest's garments, Moses records the detail of the glorious breastplate created for God's chosen one.

What are these garments called according to Exodus 39:1?

Those that wear robes of honor must look upon them as clothes of service, for from whom honor is given, service is expected. What does it say in Revelation 7:13, 15 about those arrayed in white robes?

Be sure that our armor of God is considered to be robes of honor, or holy garments, and denote service and praise.

 Back to Exodus 39:1-31 and the breastplate. What commonality do we see expressed in verses 5, 7, 21, 26, 29 and 31?

> **God participated in the creation of the breastplate of righteousness.**

This phrase is not listed in any of the previous descriptions of the priests clothing. I believe this emphasizes God's participation in the creation of the breastplate. In reading through the passage, what are some details or extravagances given to this breastplate? Try to find three.

Do you see why I liked the third breastplate description? The intricate detail to the fine construction specifically created for the wearer, blesses me. What a representation of our breastplate and place in Christ. He has taken our personalized *negative* self-righteousness and re-crafted it with His absolutely perfect *positive* righteousness. The positive overlay covered with brass was beaten to conform to the details for the wearer. Jesus was beaten and crucified so that I may wear His righteousness. Once I don His breastplate, it is decorated with fine jewels similar to the one described in Exodus 39. I shine! Well, He shines through me so brightly that I am blinding in the sunshine. And yet at this point, I am ready for service to my King. He protects my heart and all other vital organs.

If you are a believer, there is a breastplate of righteousness customized just for you. Wonder Woman's cannot even compare. Sadly, many Christians do not live as though they have been made righteous. Most walk in constant guilt and condemnation, feeling like failures and not worthy to serve God or receive anything from Him. They are hoping for a chest, when they've already been blessed with a shining, customized breastplate of righteousness. They do not realize they have been given the righteousness of Christ Jesus. We are made worthy because of Jesus. We stand tall because of His righteousness and need never to feel guilt.

 Do you ever feel guilt, condemnation or feel like you are not enough? If so, why do you think that is?

How does the belt of truth and breastplate of righteousness blend or connect? Can you wear Christ's righteousness and not His truth?

 Please be sure your prayer needs are on the **Sharpen Your Sword for Week Four.** Include beside each a verse that will encourage you as you trust God with the details.

 Review Ephesians 6:10-14. Cross out words one by one as you repeat the verses. Get the flow of these beautiful words. Copy the page for rehearsal purposes.

¹⁰ Finally, my brethren, be strong in the Lord
and in the power of His might.
¹¹ Put on the whole armor of God, that you may be able to stand
against the wiles of the devil.
¹² For we do not wrestle *against flesh and blood,*
but against principalities, against powers,
against the rulers of the darkness of this age,
against spiritual hosts of wickedness in the heavenly *places.*
¹³ Therefore take up the whole armor of God,
that you may be able to withstand in the evil day,
and having done all, to stand.
Stand therefore, having gird your loins with truth,
And having the breastplate of righteousness.
Ephesians 4:10-14

The Perfect Fit

Week Four   Day Two

Protect My Heart

"...having put on the breastplate of righteousness." Ephesians 6:14b

*I*n the previous lesson we read of the customized breastplate designed for us. Amazing! Do I hear an "Amen?" Its beauty. Its craftsmanship. Its personalization. The sacrifice provided to create it. But what about its functionality? Its purpose? Its intent?

The purpose of my hope chest was to provide a place to store treasures for future use and the purpose of our breastplate of righteousness is to provide a protection against the enemy's future attacks. We know that the devil is constantly bombarding us with missiles of lies, accusations and reminders of past sin. It's what he does. He lies, manipulates and deceives. Without the breastplate of righteousness being worn to protect us, these missiles will penetrate to our heart, our lives, and we forget the purposes of God for us.

God has a plan for your life and the enemy has a plan for your life. We must have on God's full armor so we are ready for both plans and wise enough to know the difference between them. God's purposes for our lives, spiritual victory, come to those who are prepared for battle.

> **God has a plan for your life and the enemy has a plan for your life.**

The enemy will try to talk you out of your breastplate. He will tell you, with deceitful whispers of self-talk, that you are not righteous, not worthy. He will murmur to you that you need to worry about certain situations. He will encourage you to carry your own burdens, convincing you that only you are strong enough to deal with it. He will use people that you love to hurt you and break your heart. He will cunningly convince you to remove your breastplate, allowing his accusations, hurt, burdens and worry to give you incredible heartache. When you remove the "breastplate of righteousness", you permit his arrows to strike your heart.

What is your heart? The Word of God says much about it. After all, the Maker of our heart created it. Physically, the heart is what keeps us alive. When the heart stops doing its job, we die. When it stops pumping the blood of life to all the parts of our body, we cannot continue to live. In comparison, spiritually our heart is what keeps us spiritually alive. When the heart-spirit, our emotions which control our actions, stops being controlled by the blood of Christ we cannot continue to live the abundant life. We begin to stumble and become spiritually ill because our heart is not working as it ought.

Let's do a study of the word *heart* as found in scripture. The word *heart* is written over 5,000 times in the Bible. 5,000 times!!! It can be read in 52 of the 66 books in the Bible. I have perused them all, chose many and believe from the chosen ones we can conclude a definition of a Biblical heart and why having it protected by a breastplate is so important.

Look up many of the heart references below and write a purpose or job that the heart represents or can possess. Try to find a verb, something the heart does. Then conclude why it is important to have it protected by God's righteousness.

Exodus 7:13
Exodus 35:26
Leviticus 19:17

Deuteronomy 6:5
Judges 16:18
Ruth 3:7 (the only time in this book)

1 Samuel 2:1
1 Samuel 24:5
1 Chronicles 22:19

1 Chronicles 29:17
2 Chronicles 12:14
Job 10:13

Psalm 19:14
Psalm 33:15
Psalm 34:18

Psalm 66:18
Jeremiah 17:9
Jeremiah 29:13

Matthew 5:8 (my life verse)
Luke 2:19
John 14:1

Acts 15:8
Romans 8:27
Romans 10:10
Colossians 3:15

 From your heart word study, compile a list of actions your spirit-heart can perform. List action words:

 Why must our heart be protected by the breastplate of righteousness?

Hearts are the center of our emotions, where our actions are produced. We will act, react, and respond to thoughts that we have. Those actions produce habits in our lives – good or bad. These determine the reputation and character that we develop and the life we live. Imagine having the breastplate of God's righteousness to screen our heart, center of emotions, before a wrong action is done. It would be a holy sifting of sorts.

Will our heart get hurt? Of course, it will. Will we feel defeated on occasion? Yes. But, knowing that God has purpose for us and knowing our true identity in Christ, we are able to stand tall and spiritually battle in the righteousness that God provides. Our hearts will be protected by God's truth that we are His and His plans are perfect. Satan is not fighting you because you are weak, feeble and insecure, but because he knows you have purpose. He solely desires to interfere with God's purposes and call on your life.

Do you believe you have purpose?

How does believing that determine the way your heart responds to various situations?

Use the following three verses to write a prayer to God about having the right heart.

Psalm 51:10   Psalm 19:14   Psalm 90:12

 Make it personal from your heart to His. He loves when you come to Him straight from the heart. **Sharpen your sword for Week Four.**

 Continue to work on memorizing Ephesians 6:10-14. If you have not started yet, it is not too late. Copy it down and post in various places you live life – your car, bathroom mirror, desk, refrigerator, purse, etc. Start meditating on these truths.

> **Satan is not fighting you because you are weak, fearful and insecure, but because he knows you have purpose.**

The Perfect Fit

Week Four   Day Three

The Best We Can

"...having put on the breastplate of righteousness." Ephesians 6:14b

I try to do my best. I really do try to make the right decisions when they need to be made. I believe we all do. We truly do the best we can. We observe situations and from that observation make decisions. From there, we live with the consequences and circumstances that arise. Sometimes we consult the Lord and wait for His answer. And then, other times, we feel we must make a decision without fully knowing in what direction the Lord is leading. We know what our heart is telling us and those emotions can shout loudly, can't they? But, often, we follow it without God's righteousness going before us. At that point, we are not protected from the enemy. We are on our own and out of the protection of God's righteousness. After observing the situations around them and getting sound Godly wisdom, what did the Israelites ask God's prophet Samuel for in 1 Samuel 8:19-20?

Did they heed the wisdom given by Samuel? (Look at verses 11-18)

They had looked at the surrounding circumstances, even heard wisdom from a man of God, and yet decided their rational thinking and emotions were best. They wanted a king.
Who was their king prior to this encounter? (1 Samuel 8:7)

Was the king they already had ruling with excellence?
Why did they feel they needed a new one?

Even though the Israelites stepped out from God's wisdom, protection and guidance, God allowed them to have their way. God knew what the result would be, but He understood that they would not understand unless they walked these difficult days by themselves. He tried, through Samuel, to give them truth to make a wise abundant-life decision, but they believed they knew what was best.

I can't help but use my imagination to how this played out. This is not recorded in the Bible, but think about the talk behind closed doors about wanting a king. You know there had to have been gossip sessions about Samuel getting too old to lead. Included were stretched stories, giving examples of mistakes that Samuel had already made. Can you hear them? There were conversations in dark tents about what to do and how they could fix it themselves. Finally, after enough chatter, they had convinced themselves that they were right. Of course they were. When we rally others together in secret places to our hearts desires, often they convince us we are correct. It starts as a small bubble, but after adding more steam, it becomes a volcano–not ready to listen to Godly counsel.

Anyway, God allowed them to have their way. Why? It seemed the stiff-necked people were again only listening to their own wisdom. He gave Samuel the okay to choose a king for them, after explaining the sad outcome of this poor decision (1 Samuel 8:10-18).

Similar to the Israelites, often my mind and heart decide that I feel a certain way. I'm passionate about it only to later find that I was wrong. I even rally around support from others and seek wisdom that is what I want to hear. Sadly, it is often all about me and my pride. Let's see what happened to the Israelites when they got their heart's desire despite God's leading against it.

It started out exciting. Isn't it always thrilling when we get our way or we get what we think is the desire of our hearts? God sent the prophet Samuel on a journey to get Saul.

Read 1 Samuel 9:15-16.

Samuel was a man of God. I love the line, "the LORD had told Samuel in his ear". The beauty is that Samuel listened and obeyed. Samuel had exceptional hearing. God had been whispering things to Samuel for a long time and God knew He could trust him. I love when God whispers things in my ear. When we are tuned into Him, His Spirit's voice is very clear.

Recall 1 Samuel 3. Remember Samuel's first prophecy? He was just a young boy. Read 1 Samuel 3:10 and 19. From these verses what can be determined about Samuel's childhood?

Back up one more time in the book of 1 Samuel to 1:24-27. From this passage would you conclude that Hannah, his mother, was a woman of integrity? Why or why not? Before you answer, read through the prayer of Hannah in Chapter 2:1-10.

 Do you believe Hannah's life had an influence on Samuel's willingness to listen to God?

Being a Godly woman, who wears the full armor daily, is not only so that we may be victorious and defeat the enemy, or even that we might experience abundant life, but our wearing the armor is also an investment into the future of our children. In what way do you agree with that statement?

Now, here we are in 1 Samuel 9 and Samuel is advanced in years. He had served God's people for many years by faithfully listening to God. God spoke, he listened. In chapter ten of 1 Samuel we read that Saul is proclaimed King and God's Spirit came upon Saul (10:6).

Read what Samuel has to say at Saul's Coronation in 1 Samuel 12:12-15.

Samuel states that God has given them what they asked, now what is expected of them?

The Israelites got what they wanted. Are they happy? Read 1 Samuel 12:19-25.

Often when we get what we wanted we are still not happy. We want more _____.
*money   *affection   *friends   *respect   *appreciation   *time   *vacation

Yet we know that if we had more, we would want more and still not be content. We need only more of God. He is only what will fulfill our deepest desires. God is the answer to *more*.

Saul started off as a good king. A good man. A man showered with God's spiritual blessing (1 Samuel 10:6, 9, 10). But things quickly changed. His eyes went from God and others, to himself. He began to forget that his blessings were from God. He made an unlawful sacrifice in chapter 13 where he took matters into his own hands. He began thinking apart from God, in 1 Samuel 14:19, basically saying, "I don't need God's guidance."

As a result, what happened in the next verse (v. 20) during the battle?

There was great _____. Although the Lord saved Israel that day. (v 23), Saul's dependence on himself and not God caused confusion in the battle.

Oh, the similarities to the spiritual battle we fight while dressed in the full armor. The moment we take our eyes off the LORD and His righteousness, and trust our own thinking... there is great confusion in the battle. Our heart, with our emotions, begins to rule and no longer is God's righteousness protecting us. Rather, we are protected by our own self-righteousness.

 What does God's Word say about confusion? 1 Corinthians 14:33   James 3:16

Saul continued to practice self-righteousness to rule God's people in many ways; by a rash oath to not eat (14:24-46), taking the goods for himself (14:52), and other decisions that were not according to God's righteousness. Finally, he was rejected as king. (1 Samuel 15:26)

Saul was told not to keep any goods of war, but what did he do according to 1 Samuel 15:9?

Although he was a warrior, he did not wear the armor of God, according to verse 21.

It is evident that he no longer heeded God's wisdom in 1 Samuel 15:15 when talking to Samuel he said, "… to sacrifice to your God". The Living God was no longer Saul's God and the remainder of his life showed it to be true. The Israelites and Saul are examples of self-righteousness. I confess there have been times when I have allowed self-righteousness to guide my thinking. (And sadly, there will probably be times again.) I have placed the focus on my will, and have even rallied support from others. At those moments, I was not sporting the breastplate of God's righteousness.

I shake my head in disbelief that there could be a moment in time when I would think, even for an instant, that I was more important than another. How could there be any righteousness in me apart from what God provides? I desire to keep my breastplate on and have God's heart, not mine. I want to try my best, but realize that my best will never suffice. It is God's best working in my heart that will make the difference.

Is there an area of your life where you are possibly wearing your own righteousness like a breastplate? Thinking about yourself above others and not obeying God's direction?

 Pray about it. Write in **Sharpen Your Sword for Week Four** and include a verse in support. It is the best thing you could do today.

 Continue to review Ephesians 6:10-14.

The Perfect Fit

Week Four   Day Four

Righteousness- He's done His best.

"...having put on the breastplate of righteousness." Ephesians 6:14b

What a coincidence! When we continue with the story of King Saul and the Israelites in 1 Samuel, we see God at work rearranging and working behind the scenes for what is best for his people. Obviously, the word *coincidence* is incorrect. "Coincidence with God?" I think not! God is fully aware and plans every step. And, the story gets better and better.

Chapter 15 of 1 Samuel ends in verse 35 with God stating that He regretted He had made Saul king over Israel. Some versions even go so far as to say *repented*. He had pity or contemplation over the decision He had made. One definition is *to breathe strongly*. Can't you see God heavily sighing over the situation that the Israelites and Saul had gotten into?

But God is a God of action. He had his plans for a king well before the Israelites asked for one. He had one chosen and now in 1 Samuel <u>God's plan</u> begins to play out.

Read 1 Samuel 16:1. Who chose this king?

Continue in this chapter through verse 13. It is the familiar story of Samuel choosing from Jesse's sons the next king of Israel. Samuel thought God would choose one like the predecessor, but God had other ideas.

What does verse 7 say about God's job description for a king?

> ## When self-righteousness rules, defeat is sure to follow.

Remembering that David is just a boy, what two things happen to him in verse 13?

God had a plan. He always has a plan. Often in our self-righteousness we get confused in the battle and find ourselves off the path God had planned; therefore struggling to fight the battle. His man, after His heart has now been anointed as king, but David's time to rule had not yet come.

In 1 Samuel 16:14-23 we read of King Saul's tormenting spirit. We can get into trouble when we allow our own spirit to rule. Torment. Anxiety. Depression. Rejection. When self-righteousness rules, defeat in spiritual battles is sure to follow. God's righteousness, Spirit and rule are not prevalent. The king desired a musician to calm his spirit. And whom does the servant suggest in verse 18 that he get? _____ Amazing. Coincidence? I think not! What are some of the descriptions given to David in verse 18?

Check out that last description... "and the Lord is with him."

The Lord is with those whose heart is stayed on Him. When your heart is stayed on Him, you have a heart after God's heart, and the breastplate of righteousness fits perfectly.

What three verbs, action words, apply to David in 1 Samuel 16:21?

Because David was full of the Spirit of the Lord and surrounded with God's righteousness, and not his own, he could stand, love and become. Fully dressed in the armor of God, David stood before Saul, and in that attire, he could love freely and become the man God had designed.

1 Samuel 17 tells the story of David and Goliath. This is probably one of the most memorable of all Biblical stories. Please read the entire chapter as if you've never read it before. List three new thoughts, ideas or precepts.

1.

2.

3.

Let's examine this story now thinking on God's righteousness and how we are to wear the full armor of God. I Samuel 17:5-7 lists some details of Goliath's armor.

How does it differ from the armor we are to wear?

1 Samuel 17:23-24 states that David heard for himself Goliath's slanders.
What did all the others soldiers do?

What was David's response?

The Israelite army looked like they were dressed in armor and in the world's interpretation they were. But, only David was dressed in the full armor of God. I think sometimes our churches are like that; full of people looking like they are wearing the armor of God, even fighting on the fronts, but when the time to make a choice for righteousness is upon them—they flee in fear. I'm not talking about unbelievers and believers, I'm referring to those that really desire to be in the Word versus those that just hit and miss Bible study and application. If they are not filled with the Word and allowing it to sift them, they are not dressed in the breastplate of righteousness. When the evil day comes, they will not be prepared.

Like David, we have three possible responses to fear. We can **flee**, **freeze** or **fight**. All the soldiers that day fled, yet God gives us no armor to protect our back. He doesn't expect His soldier to flee in fear; rather, go head on in Jesus' name and fight. He expects us to rest in His righteousness. He's given us the power to do so.

What word does David use to describe God in verse 26?

> **We can flee, freeze or fight.**

David knew the reality of God. He knew that in the midst of conflict, in the very heat of the battle, our God is alive and ready to fight. Trusting in God alone, and not ourselves, shows that we realize it is His righteousness in us will win the battle. Be realistic, expect a miracle.

 You are in a spiritual battle and you know the right thing to do. Then you hear it, "You are not enough." The enemy whispers that in our ear so often. Look who said that to David in verse 33. Did David listen to the enemy's whisper?

How did he combat the attack?

Are you in the midst of a trial and the enemy is whispering, "You're not enough?" The enemy is correct—we are not. But, my dear sister, God is. David knew the **reliability of God**. What does he recount in verses 34-37 that shows he is trusting God's past provision?

When we share what God has done for us personally, no one can discount it. God showed himself to us and He will again. No one can disprove or discredit our personal testimony. Understanding that, what does Saul say in verse 37b?

David knew the **resources of God**. What does King Saul offer in 1 Samuel 38-39?
Could David use them? _____ Why or why not?

Name some ways we attempt to wear someone else's spiritual armor?

David knew he had to fight this battle with the gifts, talents and abilities that God had given him. He couldn't try to be something he was not designed to be. Herein lies a good lesson for us. Let's not try to do something that we are really not called to do. If God has called you to use a slingshot, don't try to use a spear. If God has given you a passion for children, and called you to nursery work... then serve there. If God has given you a love to cook and be hospitable, then cook yourself silly in the name of Jesus. Too many are trying to use a spear when a slingshot is more their size.

David knew the **righteousness of God**. He knew God was perfect, holy, righteous and good in every way. He knew that when he rested in God's righteousness, God would honor him.

 What do the following verses state about God's Righteousness? Our self-righteousness?
Psalm 97:2   Psalm 89:14   Romans 10:2-4

When Paul mentions in Ephesians the breastplate of righteousness, first and foremost he is speaking of the righteousness of Christ, which one receives when they trust Christ as Savior. It is not our righteousness that forms the breastplate. We are protected from Satan's attacks when, by faith, we rely on Christ's righteousness. This imputed righteousness can never be taken away from us. Many of us know it to be true, trust it to be true in faith, but fail to appropriate it for ourselves. Put it on ... piece by piece. This is God's best for us.

 Like David, are there giants that you need to trust in God's righteousness about? Surrender them to God in prayer. Record in the **Sharpen Your Sword for Week Four**.

 Continue to meditate and memorize Ephesians 6:10-14. Write it below.

The Perfect Fit

Week Four   Day Five

My Breastplate of Righteousness

"...having put on the breastplate of righteousness." Ephesians 6:14b

They were just children, but the harsh words on the playground that day stung deep to the heart. "No, you can't play with us," is what she said to her classmate. Rejection was all the little girl felt. It was written all over her face and in the way she carried herself. My youngest was playing that day and overheard this conversation. Dressed in the breastplate of righteousness, my daughter immediately invited the hurt child to play. She knew by doing it, she herself would receive rejection from the cool group of girls, but she chose to do the right thing. Simply put, she chose righteousness.

As grown women, things really haven't changed all that much. Our situations and struggles seem more mature, but in reality we deal with hurt, rejection, judgment, and God-ordained opportunities to make righteous decisions. When sporting the breastplate of Christ's righteousness those decisions are much easier to make.

Understand completely that the righteousness we possess is imputed righteousness, given to us from God. It is not from us, but from God because of the faith we have in Jesus Christ. We discussed yesterday David's imputed righteousness. Although David's story is found in the Old Testament, still we see Jesus there. The author of Ephesians wrote Romans; and in Romans four, he explains imputed righteousness. This is a bit of a difficult passage, but work with me and let's hear what God is saying to us personally.

   Read Romans 4:1-4. In these verses, why was righteousness accounted to Abraham?

Read Romans 4:5-8. Here we hear from David, the very one that we studied yesterday.
Do our works have anything to do with our imputed righteousness?

What does "Blessed is the man to whom the LORD shall not impute sin." (v. 8) mean to you?

Glory! Hallelujah! My sin is not accounted to me. David rejoiced because his sin was not imputed to him either. (Please understand, David deliberately sinned; yet he was forgiven. This was written after his sin with Bathsheba.)

Read Romans 4:9-12. According to this passage, when was Abraham accounted as righteous? (Genesis 12:1-3 and Romans 4:3) Was it before or after his act of circumcision?

What does that have to do with our works and our imputed righteousness?

According to Romans 4:13, why did the promise come to Abraham?

Read Romans 4:14-22. In verse 20, what did Abraham do?

I love the line "to give glory to God"—we'll come back to that one. Now Paul transitions from Old Testament to New Testament to Today. Read Romans 4:23-25.
According to these verses, to whom is this righteousness imputed?

We've been justified by faith; now we can wear His breastplate of righteousness.
Putting on the breastplate of righteousness means more than simply standing in the righteousness of Christ. We are to give God the glory by reflecting His righteousness in our conduct and holy living. This is *imparted righteousness* and has to do with the Christian's daily walk. As we walk in the Spirit, Ephesians 5:18, the righteousness of Christ is imparted to us. The result is that we become more like Christ.
Did you know that Christ Himself wore the breastplate of righteousness? The prophet Isaiah spoke of the Messiah in Isaiah 59:16-17. What four things are mentioned of the Messiah putting on?
(1) _____ (2) _____ (3) _____ (4) _____.

He is the perfect Son of God and example to us. We are to be like him in every way.

Sister, we **need** to walk, talk and live a clean, pure, Spirit-filled life. Bottom line—it is the only way to the abundant life promised. It is the way to victory in the battles. By doing so we honor Christ and glorify His Father. We need to confess sin when the Holy Spirit brings it to our heart and mind. When righteousness is not being lived out, we

> **Sinning saints struggle to stand when the enemy attacks.**

are vulnerable to the enemy and become easy targets for his fiery darts. Sinning saints struggle to stand when the enemy attacks.

Let's end with a passage in 1 Timothy 6:11-16. It begins with "But you, O woman of God…" (Okay, it doesn't say *woman*, but in translation and application we can surely relate.)
Go ahead, read it…

What are we to pursue? (5 things)

What are we to do? (4 things)

Oh, don't I desire to be without spot. It seems I am constantly spotted with sin. Making mistakes daily like losing my cool, not forgiving, thinking poorly of someone, not spending the time in prayer and the Word, not being the helpmate I should for my husband, or the mother I should be for my children… But wait!! Before I get down on myself, I should recall from where these accusations are possibly coming. Are they lies from the enemy? Can't I do all things in Christ? Yes! I am fully aware of my imputed righteousness and imparted righteousness and I can live in it. Will I be perfect in my actions and reactions? No, but wearing the breastplate of righteousness I will strive in all ways to honor Jesus. I will stand before men by reason of His righteousness having produced righteousness in me. Such righteousness cannot be damaged by the enemy. I will wear the breastplate personally designed for me.

My personal breastplate of righteousness? I imagine myself in a beautiful white flowing gown. The bodice is covered with white shining sequins. It is not the harsh type of sequins, but very soft, tiny and smooth to the touch. It shimmers. It sparkles and light reflects off of it and shines about the room. It has a tinge of gold to coordinate perfectly my belt of truth. It is pure, because He who gave it to me is pure. It is feminine, because the Creator of the Universe has designed it perfectly for me. And as I become more like Him, and reflect His nature, it glistens the more. Dressed in His Righteousness all I can do is lift praise to His Holy Name.

Let us with Paul, in Timothy 6:15, give praise to our God.
He is blessed.
He is the only Potentate. (Great authority, mighty)

Oh, let's make it personal and direct our praise to Him directly.
You are the King of Kings.
You are the Lord of Lords.

You alone have immortality
You dwell in unapproachable Light
You have all honor,
And Everlasting Power!!!
Amen.

 Instead of just writing a prayer request today in **Sharpen You Sword for Week Four**, include a word of praise to God for His righteousness to you. Find a verse from the Psalms to match.

 Review. Recite. Review.
Do it again. Ephesians 6:10-14 is becoming a part of who you are.

Sharpen Your Sword

Week Four

Concern	Truth to Believe	Date	Answer
A worry	Proverbs 3:5-6 "He will direct my paths."		

The Perfect Fit

Week Four Wrap Up

Principal Questions for Week Four

1 .List three details or extravagances given to the breastplate in Exodus 39:1-31.

2. List some of the actions your spirit-heart can perform.

3. What does the Bible say about confusion?

1 Corinthians 14:33

James 3:16

4. What do the following verses state about God's Righteousness? Our self-righteousness?

Psalm 97:2

Psalm 89:14

Romans 10:2-4

5. Read Romans 4:1-8; what do these verses tell us about God's righteousness?

Practical Questions for Week Four

1. Why should we not incubate feelings of guilt, condemnation or that you are not enough?

2. Why must our heart be protected by the breastplate of righteousness?

3. In what way is a godly life an investment into the future of our children?

4. What can you do when the enemy whispers 'you are not enough" in our ear?

5. What does "Blessed is the man to whom the LORD shall not impute sin." (Romans 4:8) mean to you

Session Five – Gospel of Peace Shoes

"And your feet shod with the preparation of the gospel of peace;" Ephesians 6:15

Is 52:7   Roman 10:15;5:1   I Cor 15:1-4   Eph 2:14   I Thes 5:23
Phil 4:6-7   Is 57:20-21

The Roman Soldier's shoes would not be a heavy boot, but a sandal-type shoe with hob nail soles, cleat-like. They would generally have open tops. These heavy soles would protect the feet from the common military practice of planting sharpened sticks in the ground.

What is "Peace" to you? _____

Peace _____ God, granted to us at salvation. Romans 5:1

   a. The enemy cannot take this peace away.

   b. Nothing can separate us from this peace.

Peace _____ God Is 26:3

   a. If we surrender it, the enemy can take this peace from us.

   b. A settled walk that is _____

   c. Firmly planted, yet can be hindered by _____
      _____ is our Peace Ephesians 2:14

Review of Weeks 1-4

Foundation – B_____, A_____, M_____, G_____, O_____, R_____

Belt of Truth–What _____

Breastplate of Righteousness–_____ _____

Shoes of Peace–_____ I Thes 5:23-24

The Perfect Fit

Week Five   Day One

Shoe Shopping

"And your feet shod with the preparation of the gospel of peace;" Ephesians 6:15

My second daughter is a shopper. She especially loves clothes and really cute shoes. Once, when she was only three years old, we entered a shoe store to purchase sneakers. She walked in, stopped in the doorway, took a deep breath and exclaimed, "I love the smell of this place!"

Although being surrounded by shoes and the aroma of leather doesn't do anything special for me, shoes are a practical part of life and I for one can appreciate a comfortable pair. Most days, I have a very swollen left ankle and foot, so I often buy my shoes a half size larger. I feel self-conscious about my ankle size, and believe I never look good in any shoes; but I do smile at the thought of my gospel shoes of peace. They will fit me perfectly and flatter my feet and attire. How? My Heavenly Father personally designed them for me. They even fit my swollen ankle perfectly. They are Spirit-filled shoes and I glide when wearing them. Actually, there are some pretty other amazing shoes described in the Bible. Just for fun, here are a few I've discovered.

What would be a great feature about the shoes mentioned in Deuteronomy 29:5?

Do the shoes in Deuteronomy 33:25 sound like they'd be comfortable to you?

How about the description of the princess shoes in Song of Solomon 7:1?

Read Luke 15:22. What did the Father give to his son?

Who do we represent in this story?

How are the shoes significant?

In John 1:27, how are the shoes used?

Sandals, the shoes of the biblical time period, are a key part of many Biblical stories and very significant to the Christian Soldier. We are told to have our feet shod with the preparation of the gospel of peace. The shoes of the soldier were elaborately cut military sandals called *caligae*.[1] They are called boots in many references but do not resemble boots as we think of them. They were not heavy, but strong and well ventilated, with leather straps across the top. The studded soles enabled the soldier to stand firm. The soles had little pieces of metal protruding from the bottom like the cleats of a football shoe—but with an open top.

During the time of the Roman wars, there was a common military practice of planting sticks in the ground, which had been sharpened to razor-points. They were then concealed in the ground to be practically invisible. The soldier that stepped on the sharpened sticks would be completely debilitated and unable to walk if his foot was pierced, thus it proved to be a very effective tactic. Great care was taken by Rome to supply the soldiers with the appropriate footwear for the assignment. Some had toe spikes and/or built-in spurs with which to do some serious damage to the enemy. The upper part of the sandals were removable metal greaves that extended up over the kneecap protecting the knees, shins and ankles. (Greaves are protective devices for the legs.)[2]

I like a comfortable pair of shoes, but to me barefoot is best. When no shoes are on my feet, it usually spells relaxation. It means I am home to stay for a while. My guard is down and I'm in my comfort zone. If I lived that way spiritually, I would be in serious trouble. The enemy would see my relaxed-status and I would be a target for his arrows. I must be dressed in the armor, with my God-given gospel shoes on and ready to fight at all times.

 What kind of shoes do you have in your closet? High heels? Pumps? Flats? Sandals? Boots? If you were to go shoe shopping, what kind of pairs would you choose? Let's go shoe shopping through the Bible and find a pair or two that would describe your spiritual walk now and some that might describe where you desire to be. Let's shop!!!

Look up the verse, describe the shoes, and check if you would like to obtain a similar pair.

_____   "Truth Shoes"—Psalm 26:3

_____   "Liberty Shoes"—Psalm 119:45

_____   "Upright Shoes"—Psalm 15:2

_____   "Wiseman Shoes"—Proverbs 13:20

_____   "Friend Shoes"—Amos 3:3

_____   "My Own Way Shoes"—Psalm 81:12-13

_____   "Contrary Shoes"—Leviticus 26:21

_____   "Gospel Shoes"–Ephesians 6:15

 Out of all the shoe verses above, choose one favorite and write why you chose it. How can you relate to it today?

I don't know what you chose for your shoe wardrobe, but hopefully you were able to find something in the Bible's Shoe Closet that matches your belt of truth and breastplate of righteousness. Make every effort to coordinate, please!

 Please add any prayer concerns to the **Sharpen Your Swords for Week Five** at the end of this week's study. Be sure to choose a Bible verse that will encourage you to be strong in the Lord concerning this request.

 In your goal to memorize Ephesians 6:10-15, use the following page to review and meditate.

Ephesians 6:10-15

[10] Finally, my brethren, be strong in the Lord
and in the power of His might.
[11] Put on the whole armor of God, that you may be able to stand
against the wiles of the devil.
[12] For we do not wrestle *against flesh and blood,*
but against principalities, against powers,
against the rulers of the darkness of this age,
against spiritual hosts of wickedness in the heavenly *places.*
[13.] Therefore take up the whole armor of God,
that you may be able to withstand in the evil day,
and having done all, to stand.
14. Stand therefore having girded your loins with truth and
Having put on the breastplate of righteousness.
15 And having shod your feet with the preparation
of the gospel of peace.

The Perfect Fit

Week Five   Day Two

Prepared to Share

"... and having your feet shod with the preparation of the gospel of peace." Ephesians 6:15

Be Prepared. This is the Boy Scout's motto and it truly is a good one to have. Many a stressful moment could have, <u>should have</u>, been avoided if only proper preparations had been made. I only have daughters, so there is not a one that knows or lives by the Boy Scout motto. Many a Sunday morning comes along and someone cannot find something that they need to get ready for church. A shoe, stockings, Bible, etc. I hear you saying, "Well, if you had gotten everything together on Saturday night, then it would make Sunday morning less stressful." We have had successful well-organized Saturday nights, but that is not the norm. Besides, your *coulda-shoulda-wouldas* are annoying. I know that not being ready and prepared usually causes stress, but it happens. The same carries over into our spiritual life. When we are not dressed and ready to go fight the spiritual battles that come our way, stress happens. It is too late to get dressed in the armor of God after you have already been hit in battle. After being wounded, you use your energies to nurse your wounds and put together the part of your life that was injured.

When meditating on *gospel shoes* my mind goes to the book of Acts and the beginning of the Christian church. God knew what was ahead for the disciples, fellow believers and early church after Jesus resurrected from the dead and ascended into heaven. He had a purpose and calling for each man and woman in that early church, just like He does for us. God knew they would need a helper. He knew it. And so He provided a Helper in a big way.

Following the gospels, which give the account of the life of our Lord and Savior Jesus Christ, the book of Acts continues with the history of the Christian church. Let's begin in Acts 1:4-8. Read Jesus' words and then answer the following questions.

Who did Jesus provide for us according to this passage?

Why did He believe we needed Him?

Jesus promised us He would be with us always.
John 16:4-10 encourages us. How?

What will happen to us, what will we become, when the Holy Spirit comes upon us?

According to John 14:8 and Matthew 28:20, how did Jesus fulfill that promise?

After Jesus gave the promised Holy Spirit, He ascended into Heaven and now
intercedes, in prayer, for us. He died for us, sent the Holy Spirit to be with us, and continues to pray for us in Heaven. Jesus loves us more than we can even begin to imagine. Let me personalize that for a moment—Jesus loves you, beloved sister. Even if you are right now not *feeling* the love of your family, friends or church, know without a doubt that Jesus loves you and is thinking about you right now. Right at this moment. Know it and rest in it. His love has been well thought through and is with you to the end of time.

And like that is not enough, what does Acts 1:11 explain will happen?

**You are loved. I am loved. We are loved and accounted as precious by the
Creator of the Universe. Let that sink in. You are His. He is yours.**

Brace yourself and get ready for a great wind. Like the whirlwind that we discussed in week two, this one also brings opportunity to grow and be stretched. The whirlwind filled with difficulties causes us to trust our Savior, whereas this whirlwind of Acts two, provides the strength we need to not only survive difficulties, but to thrive and flourish in them. Abundant life stuff. Let's hear the wind blow in Acts 2:1-4. Go ahead and read it.

I love the expectancy of verse one. They were in one accord and ready to be amazed. They heard Jesus' promise. The believed it. And they were with confidence waiting. The promise arrived in verse two—the wind. Again the blessing comes in a wind. I think we are seeing a pattern here.

Let's not look with dreary eyes when the storms come. There very well could be a blessing hidden within. Be ready! Be expectant. Be ready. Be prepared to be amazed. Do you think it was what they expected?

> **Be prepared and be amazed.**

Would you have expected the Holy Spirit to come as He did?

And isn't that just like the LORD to not give us what we expect, but so much more.

 Verse three states that *one sat upon each of them.* The fairness of that is staggering. What does Acts 5:29-32 say about this?

Do you think some were more deserving than others?

Don't even go there in your thoughts. That would insinuate that there was even one there that *deserved* the gift of the Holy Spirit. No one deserves God's gifts. They are just that–gifts.

And then verse four says, "...*all were filled.*"

We may look around at our brothers and sisters in the faith and feel that they have more of the Holy Spirit than we do. We all have the same amount given to us at salvation; it's just that some faithful believers have learned to surrender themselves and their lives to the Lord Jesus. They daily allow the Holy Spirit to reign in their lives. They have learned to put on the full armor of God and like David, surrender the battle to God.

Remember what David told Goliath in 1 Samuel 17:47?

 How are *knowing that "the battle is the Lord's"* and *"being filled with the Holy Spirit"* the same? How are they different?

We were not in Jerusalem on the Day of Pentecost, as described in Acts two, so how can we be filled with the Holy Spirit? Do you know? How?

I know that when I trust Christ as my Savior, the Holy Spirit dwells in me. Read Romans 8:9-17.

What is stated in these verses that proves the Spirit of Christ, or the Spirit of God, or the Holy Spirit (all three are the same person) dwells in you?

What are we promised if we live by the Spirit? (v. 14)

And once we are filed with the Spirit, what works will He do within me? Following each verse, name something the Spirit will do in your life personally. *See answers below.

Acts 8:29 _____

1 John 2:27 _____

Romans 8:26 _____

John 14:16 _____

1 Thessalonians 2:13 _____

John 16:8 _____

Some possible answers for the above are (not in order): He will convict me and make me aware of my sin. He will guide me. He will intercede in prayer for me. He will teach me. He will comfort me. He will sanctify me.

As you read each passage, which area of your life do you need to surrender over to the Holy Spirit's control? How can the Spirit of God prepare you for today?

 Make it your prayer. Add it to the **Sharpen Your Swords for Week Five.**

During wartime, soldiers at the battlefront slept with their shoes on. This way they were ready to spring into action immediately. A soldier who does not have his shoes on will waste time getting prepared. God has provided for us the Holy Spirit to have us ready for action immediately. He is our preparation. When we are full of the Spirit, we are ready. And, once ready, what does Acts 1:8 and Acts 4:31 say the Holy Spirit will help us to do?

 When prepared, we have on the gospel shoes and great things will happen. With expectancy, we will look at that tomorrow.

Complete this verse. Ephesians 6:15. "…and having …"

The Perfect Fit

Week Five   Day Three

A Bounce in Your Step

"...and having shod your feet with the preparation of the gospel of peace." Ephesians 6:15

Recently, I had the joy of watching my youngest in her first, and probably last, dance recital. I have experience as a dance recital mom. My oldest danced many years ago. But my youngest is not the elegant ballerina her sister used to be. No, she is the *hip-hop girl*. She likes to jam and jive to the music. She likes music with a strong beat. She swings her hips, lifts her arms, and *feels* the music. It sounds risqué in writing, but it is quite innocent and exciting to watch. The girl has got some rhythm. The energy in her eyes, her toes, and the room is high.

I can only imagine the high energy level in the early part of the book of Acts. As we read yesterday the promised Holy Spirit came and He empowered the disciples and early church. Immediately, following the coming of the Holy Spirit, Peter spoke and there was vital church growth. (Acts 2) Acts 3 tells the story of Peter and John and what happens when the Holy Spirit is given authority to rule and reign. God provides the Holy Spirit so we can be prepared to walk in His ways, doing His will, wearing the Shoes of Peace. Let's see what happened when Peter and John walk in the Lord's will.

Read Acts 3:1. While full of the Holy Spirit, where were Peter and John headed?
How do you find that to be significant?

Once we are full of the Spirit of God we desire to be in communication with God. But I find it interesting that they were headed to the temple or church. Do you think the local church is important to our spiritual growth? In what ways?

Filled with and walking in the Spirit, we desire to be in fellowship with the local church.

Read Acts 3:2-4. The lame man enters, sees the two disciples, and asks for alms. What does Peter say to him?

With that simple three-word statement they gave him respect and worth. Looking someone in the eyes in love is often challenging. If I am feeling humbled by a situation or circumstance, or even belittled by someone, looking directly into the eyes takes effort. Immediately following a time of correction with our daughters, I deliberately make eye contact with them to reassure my love for them. There is power and respect in eye contact. It affirms them and gives them worth.

> # There is power and respect in eye contact.

Filled with and walking in the Spirit, we give others worth.

Let's continue with Acts 3:5-6. What did the man expect them to give him? What did they offer him?

So many times we pray for God to meet our needs, and money is often the only answer that works for us. But God is such a creative God and thinks outside the box. Don't limit Him. He sees the whole picture and will meet our needs, but usually in a most unusual way. And I can promise you, it will be the hand out we were looking for! When it works in a God way, He gets all the glory. Then we know the Holy Spirit is at work and we are walking in our gospel shoes. Notice that they gave all the glory and *credit* to the Lord Jesus, *in the name of Jesus of Nazareth.* It really doesn't matter who gets the credit, as long as God gets the glory.

Filled with and walking in the Spirit, we see God at work.

In Acts 3:7 the two disciples acted in obedience to what God directed. What two verbs describe what they did?

 When is the last time you took someone by the hand in the name of Jesus?

The end result is always *lifting them up.* They walked to the lame man because he could not walk himself and lifted him in the power and name of Jesus. I usually do not have excess funds to bless others with, but given in the power of the Holy Spirit, there are many other ways I can *lift them up.*

List as many ways as you can to encourage others in the name of Jesus.

God asks us to give what we have in *the power of His might.* We all have a listening ear, closed lips to hold a secret, a prayer, a card in the mail, a text, a phone call or an encouraging word. We can probably all remember receiving a card in the mail at just the needed moment. Now, that's a

God-thing. When the timing is superb and your heart and spirit is lifted, know the Holy Spirit was using someone to bless you. The Holy Spirit in us causes the Holy Spirit to rise in others. You immediately *receive strength* (v. 7).

Filled with and walking in the Spirit, we lift and strengthen others.
The real action occurs in verse 8, what four different words show the action the lame man demonstrated?

This is exciting stuff! This tender story shows the progression of what wearing the full armor of God does for us. We first STAND. (We've been reminded of this three times already in the Ephesians 6 passage.) Then we WALK. That is what our shoes are for–to walk in the Spirit. Once filled with the Spirit of the Living God, we LEAP–I don't know about you, but that's pretty close to dancing to me. Dancing in the Spirit of God.

David did. What does it say in 2 Samuel 6:14?

And finally, after standing, walking, and dancing in the Spirit, we PRAISE God. The lame man did–and right in church. He was not only healed but also full of the Spirit of God.

Filled with and walking in the Spirit, we praise God. Hallelujah!

Let's finish the healing with Acts 3:9-10.
Read it and then answer the questions.
Was there any doubt who was healed?

> **Stand.**
> **Walk.**
> **Leap.**
> **Praise God.**

Was the lame man reluctant that others see his enthusiasm?
Have you even been reluctant to let others see your enthusiasm when God is at work in your life?
Would you say the man was a witness?
What did his testimony cause the others to do?

Filled with and walking in the Spirit, we cause others to be amazed at our God.

The healing is complete, but the *fall out* of the story of the lame man continues in Acts 3:11-26. Read on, Sister!

Others see what happened and Peter is filled with boldness and begins preaching to the people. I love verse 12b. Can't you hear Peter's question to the crowd? His shock, yet tongue in cheek comment to them? If there was any question on where the power came for this healing, Peter cleared it up. Peter knew where the strength came from and he wanted everyone else to know also. From where did it come?

In the name of Jesus came healing and *perfect soundness.* In your own words, how would you describe, *perfect soundness?*

Did your description/definition include the word *peace*? Mine does. The man had perfect peace because he had gospel dancing shoes on. Tomorrow we will be looking at peace carefully, but what does perfect peace mean to you?

Filled with and walking in the Spirit, we are filled with peace.

Oh, if the story were to end there, but it never does because the enemy of our souls does not want us filled and walking in the Spirit. The opposition begins in Acts 4. Read 4:1-4. Peter and John spent the night in jail for this healing. Who put him there?

Would you say that Satan was working through these people?

Filled with and walking in the Spirit, the enemy will try to defeat us.

Let's skip a bit to Acts 4:13-22. What were Peter and John told they could not do?
Do you believe this was Satan still shooting arrows their way?
What did Peter and John say in verse 20?

Filled with and walking in the Spirit, we are filled with boldness that the enemy cannot deter.

Now to finally finish the story in Acts 4:23-31. After the attacks of the enemy, they might have been discouraged a bit and needed to be refreshed in the Spirit.
Who did they go to for strength? (v. 23)

What did they corporately decide to do? (v. 24)

They could have formed a committee and discussed better ways of handling this type of circumstance. After all, this was the first miracle that brought such contention. But they chose to pray first. They prayed for boldness. They decided to wait on the Lord to renew their strength.

Filled with and walking in the Spirit, we look first to God to solve our problems.

There have been 10 different benefits to being filled with and walking in the Spirit of God with our gospel shoes. Review them and choose two that you desire for a current situation you are in.

 Make them as a prayer in **Sharpen Your Swords for Week Five** and include a verse from Acts.

 Put your shoes on and see if you have a new bounce in your step as you review Ephesians 6:10-15. Who knows? You might even break out into a dance of praise.

The Perfect Fit

Week Five   Day Four

"Wanna Hear Some Good News?"

"...and having shod your feed with the preparation of the gospel of peace" Ephesians 6:15

"Mom, I've got some good news and bad news. Which do you want first?" Now there's a loaded question. How things are at the moment determine my reply. Well, I have some good news and bad news for you today and I am choosing to give the bad news first. Here it is—we are enemies of God. We are full of sin and cannot enter His perfect, holy presence. On our own, we are destined to Hell. But there is good news—it is the gospel of Jesus Christ. Jesus is God's Son. He was born in Bethlehem, died on the cross in our place and rose victoriously from the grave. Jesus conquered death, made a way for us to gain eternal life, and the Holy Spirit provides God's presence with us all the time. The news doesn't get any better than that. The word *gospel* actually means *good news.*

We've defined gospel, but what about *gospel of peace*? This describes our shoes of peace. Look up the following verses and explain what you think they mean.

Isaiah 52:7   Romans 10:15b

Taking your gospel shoes and having your feet shod with the preparation of the gospel of peace is interpreted by many to mean witnessing. How do you think each of the previous verses have to do with witnessing and preaching?

Do you believe that our sharing our faith story with another can strengthen our walk with the Lord? How?

Peace is necessary for anyone to be an effective witness. Because of this, Satan is out to destroy the peace in our hearts by causing us to doubt and

> **Satan is out to destroy the peace in our hearts by causing us to doubt and worry.**

worry. When this happens, we are in turmoil of the soul. Therefore, a piece of the armor is provided to allow us walk peacefully.

There are two different kinds of peace spoken of in the New Testament–peace *with* God and the peace *of* God. Both are needed to have a settled walk with Christ and to witness with confidence and assurance.[1]

Read Romans 5:1-11. List five descriptions of us before we are saved.

Did you catch verse 10? We were at war with God, but what does verse 1 tell us?

 We are now at <u>peace *with* God</u>. This is permanent and promised to us at the very moment of salvation. Do you believe Satan can take our peace *with* God away? Explain. Prove it using 2 Corinthians 5:17-20 and Colossians 1:20.

The Christian soldier's readiness and firm foundation is first of all peace between himself and God. Remember, at the moment of salvation the Holy Spirit is ours. It is ours and nothing, not even spiritual wickedness in high places can take it away.

The other kind of peace is <u>peace *of* God</u>. Not only is there peace *with* God, there is the peace *of* God that enables us to stand apart from the world on a firm footing. One of my swords that I pull out often to fight the enemy is Philippians 4:6-7. When I find myself in a stressful situation, or feeling anxiousness coming upon me, I remember the sword that I can use to defeat the enemy. I even find myself praying parts of it often. According to Philippians 4:6-7, what are the steps we need to take to sense the peace *of* God keeping our heart and mind? (I like to think of this as ways to lace up our shoes of peace.)

The peace *with* God is given to us at Salvation, but the peace *of* God is an experiential peace that comes about as we live a life of complete surrender, trust and obedience to God and His Word. The peace *of* God in our everyday is just one of the many incredible blessings given to us as believers. It is the abundant life promised in John 10:10. Eternal life in Heaven is ours and I am looking forward to that day I see Jesus' face. What a promise and peace we possess knowing that our eternity is secure. But, what about the benefits of being a believer while we are still breathing on this earth? That's where the peace *of* God comes in. Think about situations throughout your day where you struggle with being calm, still, and at peace. Name a few.

Let me add several to trigger your memory: getting the kids ready for school, doing the home-work, fear of being alone, pressure with a deadline at work, or cleaning the house again with no help from the family. Does your *peace* slip away during these occasions?

Well, perhaps you've conquered these little frustrations. Perhaps you are so full of the Spirit of God that these situations do not bring you anxiety. (Or perhaps you live alone and have no work pressures. Don't get proud quite yet.) It is true that the more we walk with the Lord, read His Word and allow His Spirit to rule and reign, the better we become at handling these struggles in the victory provided for us in the full armor of God. We grow in our faith and walk. But once we *conquer in Jesus' name* the simple battles, it seems the challenges become greater. Remember, the enemy knows our weaknesses and aims, very precisely, at our weakest points.

How's your personal peace on those occasions when someone you love is mistreated? How about when you lose your job unfairly? How's your peace when a diagnosis of cancer is looming on your horizon? When your husband has an affair? When your teenage daughter announces to you that she's pregnant? When you hear the news of a terrible tragedy to a close friend or family member? You fill in the blank. When the winds are blowing strong we sometimes feel our firm footing slipping out from under us. "Where's the peace in this storm?" we might ask. And yet, those of us that have walked with the Lord for a while, and have seen Him rescue us again and again, can still have peace in the midst of these storms. We can have the peace *of* God cover us like a blanket. Tucking us in on all sides.

Often we experience peace in the big storms, but it's the little ones trip us up. I find that true in my life. I was reminded of this during the *whirlwind* season that I mentioned in Week Two. Eight days after my daughter's surgery, I was to attend a women's retreat with my church. My heart did not really want to go, but my husband, knowing the stress I'd been under, encouraged me to attend. I drug my feet in packing the car that Friday. I wanted to stay home and care for our daughter, but my husband assured me that he had everything under control. I needed to trust him. My body was in Lancaster County, Pennsylvania, but my heart, mind and soul were in southern New Jersey–that was until Saturday morning. While walking alone, very early in the morning, I found a working windmill. I firmly believe God led me to it. I stood by it, watching carefully. It was pumping water from a deep well beside a lovely pond. As it pumped up and down, water would gracefully flow into the pond down a waterfall made of rocks. The large windmill arms, propellers, were slowly and steadily doing their rotations. I was captivated by it. I sat, listening to the waterfall and the squeaking of the pump. I couldn't help but notice that the more the wind blew, the harder the pump pumped, and the more beautiful and refreshing was the waterfall.

The peace *of* God is like that windmill. The winds of trials were blowing, but the stronger they blew the harder the Spirit of God pumped peace into my life. Like water, the Holy Spirit, flowed from me. It was miraculous. It was not of my doing. No way! Yes, I squeaked and even whined some, but God in His mercy continued to pump peace into my life. He reminded me that it was in the storm that He spoke to Job, and that He had a great work to do in my life for me. I wanted the *everyday* of this season to glorify Him–in the *little things*. I wanted the result of this whirlwind season to be a testimony of how God supplies peace amidst the storm. It was the peace *of* God that was provided for me in that moment. When the whirlwinds of life begin to blow, remember that God's promises are true and meditate on them.

Unbelievers are not at peace with God, and it is impossible for them to experience the peace of God as a reality in their everyday life. But as believers, we will experience peace in proportion to the room we give the Holy Spirit in our hearts.

Another favorite peace verse that I use as a sword to fight the enemy is Isaiah 26:3. (This is another way to lace up those shoes of peace.)

What kind of peace is provided? _____ How can we obtain it? _____

When we obtain peace *with* God, the peace *of* God is ours for the asking and receiving. And when we practice the peace *of* God regularly in our lives, the gospel of peace is preached loud and clear in everything we do and say. It is a transition that naturally takes place as we grow in the Word and trust God with our trials. This is good news!

 Are there issues in life that are trying to steal your peace? Write them down as prayer requests on the **Sharpen Your Sword for Week Five**. Include a verse on peace.

 Ephesians 6:10-15 is becoming a part of you. Continue on, Soldier Girl!
(If you have not started yet, I've got good news for you. You can begin today.)

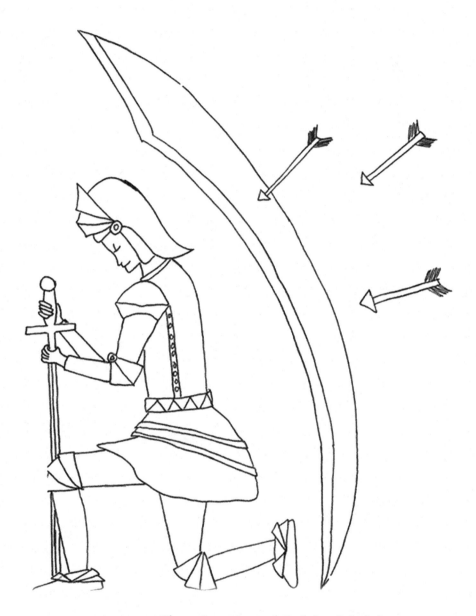

**Above all, take the shield of faith,
with which you will be able to
quench all the fiery darts of the wicked one.**

The Perfect Fit

Week Five   Day Five

My Shoes of Peace

"… and having shod your feet with the preparation of the gospel of peace." Ephesians 6:15

When I was in third grade I remember writing a story and drawing a picture of what I wanted to be when I grew up. I wrote it on the large newsprint-type paper with the top half blank and the bottom half lined with dashes for upper and lower case lettering. I'm sure you remember the paper. I wrote that I wanted to be a ballerina.

Looking back, I have no idea why I chose a ballerina. I never took a ballet lesson in my life! And that was for good reason. I was not known for being graceful and elegant. I was more the marching, climbing, football-in-the-park kind of girl. Don't get me wrong, I liked to dance for fun. But on my toes? To the music? With strength, beauty and grace? No way! Not me!

I have always admired the strength and femininity of the ballerina. Their appearance carries such magnificence. Ballerinas are such trained athletes with toned muscular bodies yet know how to carry themselves with such grace and elegance. They seem to float on air. Their costumes add to the ambiance by surrounding the dancer with fluidity of movement.

And the ballet dancer's shoes are a work of art. They are designed to fit the artist's foot perfectly, like a smooth glove. The slippers are comfortable and form fitting; yet protective enough to support the dancer's every move, total weight and safe landings. Without the proper footwear the gifted artist would slip and stumble.

My gospel shoes of peace resemble ballet slippers and when I walk in the Spirit of the Living God I am full of grace, strong and in-step with God's will. I am reminded of Miriam, Moses' sister. Immediately following the crossing of the Red Sea, the Israelites sand songs of praise to the Lord. Exodus 15:1-18 records the songs they sang. In my imagination I can hear the music, smell the salty air and feel God's miraculous victory. It must have been an unforgettable moment to behold. Life was in complete disorder and chaos for the Israelites as thy survived slavery, the plagues, escaping

Egypt and then GOD HAPPENED. God miraculously brought them to dry land and abolished their enemy. He still does that today. He brings order to our chaos and defeats our enemy. The Israelites lifted songs of worship and praise.

 Read Exodus 15:1-19. List two phrases that encourage you today. Give the reference for each.

One of my favorites is Exodus 15:8. "And with the last of your nostrils the waters were gathered together. The floods stood upright like a heap; the depths congealed in the heart of the sea." I smile at the thought of God *sneezing* my troubles away. He's so powerful.

We can feel the celebration in this song. And so did Miriam. She finds herself with all the Israelites as they cross the Red Sea. Miriam had watched her little brother mature into this man of God that led her people to freedom. She had been there when he was the baby floating in the basket down the Nile River (Exodus 2:1-10). She must had followed Moses' spiritual journey as he fled to Midian, returned to Egypt, encountered Pharaoh and survived the plagues. Now she stood by his side, victoriously saved by God's mighty Hand.

I want you to think about her feet. They were possibly barefoot from the wet sand or covered with small sandals. At any rate, they were covered with shoes of peace. Read Exodus 15:20-21. What did Miriam do in those shoes? _____ They were *praisin' feet*. She was not only walking in the Spirit of God, but full out dancing in sheer worship for His goodness.

 Read Galatians 5:16-26. When walking in the Spirit of God what will we not fulfill? (v. 16)

What are some of the works of the flesh that you personally struggle? (v. 19-21)

What are some of the works of the Spirit we will do when we walk with our shoes of peace on our feet? (v. 26)

When we walk in the Spirit of God, in obedience to Him, it is like a dance where He is leading. We are following His lead in full surrender. Galatians 5:18 even uses the phrase, "if you are led by the Spirit." Join the dance, let Him lead and follow.

When I walk in peace, after being prepared by the Holy Spirit, I am used by God in my life and in the life of others. My shoes of peace fit me perfectly. They are elegant and sparkle of white soft sequence. They match my breastplate of righteousness. Talk about coordinated! After all, they are made by the same Designer. They don't look like the Roman military boots, or sandals, at all; they are ballet slippers. And when I wear them, I am light on my feet. There's a delightful bounce in my step, yet a focused path to travel. This God-confident, sure-footed, graceful walk exemplifies peace. A God-given peace reigns – for Jesus is my peace. He is Peace himself. And I am complimented when I walk in Him.

I honor Jesus Christ when I have my shoes of peace on. I lace them up by consistently showing others Christ, especially my family, in the everyday of life. I choose to walk in a pat of service to them. As I walk the path of peace God has planned for me, He directs me to make good decisions that prepare me for difficult days ahead. The Holy Spirit guides me and prepares me for whatever is God's will for me, when I obey His call. My shoes of peace lead me to create a home of peace for my husband and family.

Can you hear the music? I can. It is lovely praise and worship music and my feet, shod with the preparation of the gospel of peace, cannot help but move to the rhythm of the beat. It's as if the pulse of God's heart is beating the rhythm and my shoes of peace obey the invitation of the music. It flows with such splendor and charm. Full of God's Spirit, every part of me exquisitely dances to the music. Oh, Beloved, Dance with Him today. Let Him lead. Just lean your head on His chest, listen to His heartbeat and follow.

 As you **Sharpen Your Swords for Week Five**, simply add a praise. Tell God how much you love being His daughter.

 Continue to dance through Ephesians 6:10-15 in your memory work. Dance through every word.

"Footprints with a Twist" is one of my favorite stories. The author is unknown.

Footprints with a Twist

Imagine you and the Lord Jesus are walking down the beach together. For much of the way, the Lord's footprints go along steadily, consistently, rarely varying the pace. But your footprints are a disorganized stream of zigzag starts, stops, turnarounds, circles, departures and returns.

For much of the way, it seems to go like this, but gradually your footprints, come more in line with the Lord's, soon paralleling His consistently. You and Jesus are walking as true friends.

This seems perfect, but then an interesting thing happens; your footprints, the ones etched in the sand next to Jesus', are now walking precisely in His steps. Inside His larger footprints are your smaller ones; safely you and Jesus are becoming one. This goes on for many miles, but gradually you notice another change.

The footprints inside the large footprints seem to grow larger. Eventually they disappear altogether. There is only one set of footprints; they have become one. This goes on and on for a long time, but suddenly the second set of footprints is back. This time it seems even worse! Zigzags all over the place. Stops ... starts ... deep gashes in the sand. A veritable mess of prints. You are amazed and shocked. Your dream ends.

Now you pray, *"Lord, I understand the first scene with the zigzags and fits. I was a new Christian; I was just learning. But you walked on through the storm ad helped me learn to walk with you."*

"That is correct."

"And when the smaller footprints were inside of Yours, I was actually learning to walk in Your steps to follow you very closely."

"Very good. You have understood everything so far."

"When the smaller footprints grew and filled in yours, I suppose that I was becoming like you in every way."

"Precisely."

"So, Lord, was there a regression or something? The footprints separated and this time it was worse than at first."

There is a pause as the Lord answers with a smile in His voice. "You didn't know? That was when we danced."

The Perfect Fit

Sharpen Your Sword

Week Five

Concern	Truth to Believe	Date	Answer
A worry	Proverbs 3:5-6 "He will direct my paths."		

The Perfect Fit

Week Five Wrap Up

Principal Questions for Week Five

1. Look up the verse and describe the shoes.

Psalm 26:3

Psalm 119:45

Psalm 15:2

Proverbs 13:20

Amos 3:3

Psalm 81:12-13

Leviticus 26:21

Ephesians 6:15

2. What does Acts 5:29-32 say about God's 'fairness?'

3. Based on Acts 3, how important do you think the local church is to our spiritual growth?

4. Can Satan take our peace *with* God away? (2 Corinthians 5:17-20 and Colossians 1:20-25.)

5. When walking in the Spirit of God, Galatians 5:16-26, what will we not fulfill?

Practical Questions for Week Five

1. How can you relate your favorite shoe verse to your life?

2. How does knowing that *the battle is the Lord's* change your world view?

3. How do you encourage others in the name of Jesus?

4. When do you primarily struggle with being calm, still, and at peace?

5. List two phrases from Exodus 15:1-19 that encourage you?

Session Six – Shield of Faith

"Above all, taking the <u>shield of faith</u>, with which you will be able to quench all the <u>fiery darts</u> of the wicked one." Ephesians 6:16

2 Sam 22:31   Psalm   7:10, 13 Psalm   18:2, 35   Psalm 3:3   Psalm 28:7
Psalm 33:20   Psalm 46:9   Psalm 76:3

The Roman Soldier's shield would have been covered with leather and placed in water. The moisture would put out the enemy's fiery darts.

What is "Faith" to you?

Faith is needed for _____ John 3:16 Ephesians 2:8

A – Admit Sin B – Believe Jesus C – Commit Life

Faith in God, simply _____

Confidence, Assurance, Immediate response

God is our _____ Gen 15:1

"God is our shield, but only as we lay hold of Him does He become our _____ against the fiery darts of the enemy. Faith must be appropriated, then it can be used. It is not true faith unless it is at work."

"True faith is always active." James 2:20

The Fiery Darts	Shield of Faith
COMPLAINING _____	Phil 2:14
WORRY _____	Matt 11:28-29
ANXIETY _____	John 16:33
CONDEMNING OTHERS _____	Col 3:12, 13
BEING RUDE _____	Titus 3:2
DISCOURAGEMENT _____ & _____	Deut. 31:8
ANGER (Impatience) _____	2 Tim 2:24
JEALOUSY _____	James 3:16-17
GOSSIP _____	Prov. 20:19
SHAME _____	Acts 3:19
FEAR _____	I John 4:18
LIES _____	Proverbs 14:25
SELF PITY _____	Eph 5:19-20

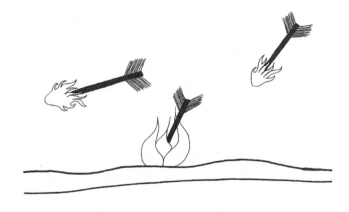

The Perfect Fit

Week Six   Day One

"Above All, Take the Shield"

"Above all, taking the shield of faith where with you will be able to quench all the fiery darts of the wicked." Ephesians 6:16

Here we are half way through the study, half way through the armor pieces of God, and Paul puts an *Above all* in there. *Above all* stresses some importance. *Above all* carries some weight. Imagine it. (And allow my imagination to embellish a bit.) Paul is possibly sitting in his home under house arrest; attached to him is a Roman soldier. He is writing this letter to the Ephesians so they might fulfill God's overall purpose for the church: to bring praise and glory to Himself. He has almost finished the letter and begins to give the analogy of the full armor of God. He starts discussing the enemy, shares the need for knowing the truth and the Truth (belt), encourages them to stand in the righteousness of God through Christ (breastplate), and challenges them to be ready with gospel shoes of peace (sandals). He pauses to reflect and his eye catches the soldier's shield that was leaning against the wall. It is very large and practically covers the entire soldier when in battle position. And Paul thinks to himself... "Faith. It must be surrounded with faith." And then he continues to write... "Above all, taking the shield of faith..."

The mood changes a bit here and the verb changes also, from *having* to *taking*. The first three pieces of the armor, Paul saw the soldier wearing, were *having* your loins girded, *having* on the breastplate, and *having* your feet shod. *Having* refers to the parts of the armor not to be taken off, but to be left on permanently. The soldier would not take off his breastplate, his belt, or his shoes, even in the lull of a battle. *Taking* refers to grabbing immediately. The last three pieces: the shield, helmet and sword must be taken up quickly–possibly, when warfare begins. They must be prepared and ready for use. They cannot be damaged and broken when needed for battle. Your faith, salvation and use of the sword should be in excellent condition and perfect working order.

Above all suggests importance and priority, as if faith is more important than the other pieces mentioned. It indicates that the shield of faith is vital for our protection. The shield did serve as protection for the entire body. All the parts of the armor by themselves will never be able to protect the soldier in battle. Without faith (or the shield), he was vulnerable.

 "Above all." This phrase is throughout scripture and each time it carries significance. What are we to do above all in the following verses?

1 Chronicles 16:25 _____

Colossians 3:14 _____

Ephesians 6:16 _____

Out of these three, which do you need to make a priority, *above all*, in *your* life?

Who is *above all* in the following verses?

Deuteronomy 7:14 _____

Exodus 19:5 _____

Psalm 95:3 _____

Psalm 135:5 _____

John 3:31 _____

Were you surprised by who was above all in the first two verses from Deuteronomy and Exodus? I was. I shake my head in wonder when I consider it. How does that truth make you feel?

Most of our days, I think, we live as though we are above all. It is our sinful nature to think of ourselves and what pleases us. It's the *All about me* mentality that rules and reigns in our lives. It's nothing new. I do believe as mothers, most of us women don't possess the *All about me,* all the time. It's just not *mom* material. We naturally put our children and husband's needs ahead of ourselves. It's just what we do. *But there are seasons,* when my personal pity parties outnumber the random acts of kindness done toward my family.

> **My personal pity parties often outnumber my random acts of kindness.**

When I'm having a pity party, I'm always bewildered that no one in my family wants to show up and *party* with me. I invite them, but they decline. I guess they'd prefer to go to the party that is *all about them*. It is then that I need to practice *The Pause* and think on the fact that *above all* means that it is really *all about Him* and what He desires of me. It's then I need to rest behind my shield of faith and reflect on the fact that it is *all about Him*.

He gave Himself for me. He loved me when I was, and am, unlovable. He intercedes on my behalf. It is truly all about Him. He is *above all*. But the beauty is, He thinks it is all about me. Look back at Deuteronomy 7:14 and Exodus 19:5. We are His treasure. He places us *above all*. When our faith is in focus, He is above all and we understand that He places us *above all*. This is faith in focus and in action. This is the personal relationship that we share with the Creator of the Universe. He thinks on us whether we think on Him or not. Our shield of faith gets strengthened when we meditate on His Word and the promises in there for us. It's a win-win situation for us.

Michael W Smith wrote a song entitled "Above All". If you know the melody, sing it as worship to your King today. (And, if you don't know the tune, make up your own.) I challenge you to sing it out loud in sheer worship. If you dare, why don't you put on your shoes of peace and dance along. As you sing in worship, setting Him *above all* in your life, imagine your damaged shield of faith being repaired. The arrows that have dented it and the fear that has weakened it cannot stand in the presence of the Holy One.

Above All
by Michael W. Smith

Above all powers, Above all kings
Above all nature and all created things
Above all wisdom and all the ways of man
You were here before the world began
Above all kingdoms, Above all thrones
Above all wonders the world has ever known
Above all wealth and treasures of the earth
There's no way to measure what you're worth
Crucified, Laid behind the stone
You lived to die, Rejected and alone
Like a rose trampled on the ground, You took the fall
And thought of me, Above all

 Praise replaces fear with faith. Worship Him, above all. Let your worship be your prayer today. Record in **Sharpen Your Sword for Week Six**.

 Add verse 16, and continue to work on Ephesians 6:10-16.

[10] Finally, my brethren, be strong in the Lord

and in the power of His might.

[11] Put on the whole armor of God, that you may be able to stand

against the wiles of the devil.

[12] For we do not wrestle *against flesh and blood,*

but against principalities, against powers,

against the rulers of the darkness of this age,

against spiritual hosts of wickedness in the heavenly *places.*

[13.] Therefore take up the whole armor of God,

that you may be able to withstand in the evil day,

and having done all, to stand.

14. Stand therefore having girded your loins with truth and

Having put on the breastplate of righteousness.

15. And having shod your feet with the preparation

of the gospel of peace.

16. Above all, take the shield of faith,

with which you will be able to

quench all the fiery darts of the wicked one.

The Perfect Fit

Week Six   Day Two

Enlisted into the Lord's Army and Ready to Fight!

"Above all, taking the shield of faith where with ye shall be able to quench
all the fiery darts of the wicked." Ephesians 6:16

I can hear the children singing with such enthusiasm – and as they sing their legs are marching, arms are riding, shooting and soaring.

"I may never march in the infantry
Ride in the Calvary
Shoot the artillery
I may never soar o'er the enemy
But I'm in the Lord's Army
YES, SIR!"

The Lord's Army was one of my girls' favorite Sunday school songs and they sang it with all their hearts ... and all of their lungs on the '*Yes, Sir!*' part. It's a cute children's song, but when we reflect on what it *truly means* to be in the Lord's army, there's nothing *cute* about it. It's wrestling with and shooting artillery at the enemy. It's knowing you will be victorious and always being prepared to fight and win. It's being wounded in battle. It's strategizing your next move. It's obeying without question the authority over you. It's bloody. It hurts. It's lonely. It's war!

As I write, our nation is at war against terrorism. I have wept and prayed for young men and women serving our country in this horrible war. I'm sure you have also. Some of them enlisted knowing the danger that was possibly and probably theirs. Others had lofty dreams of ambition and glory, only to realize the horrors of combat. I have never served our country in the military, but

I am sure what one survives in the midst of war could never be properly anticipated. They simply must be ready for anything.

To this point, Sisters, we have discussed being a woman of truth, only after knowing Truth Himself, Jesus Christ. (Belt) We have looked at examples of imputed and imparted righteousness, knowing it is only through Christ's righteousness that we can do any good thing. (Breastplate) We have learned to walk *in* the peace of God, only after we have made the decision to make peace *with* God. (Shoes) Each of these pieces of armor is ours to wear daily, after we appropriate them. We have enlisted in the Lord's army and we are learning to be soldiers that would bring Him glory by living God-honoring lives in His Spirit. It's as if we have been in boot camp and *learned about* the battle, some of our resources and the importance of full surrender in obedience to our Commander-in-Chief, Jesus Christ. We've practiced strategies to defeat the enemy and we are waiting for the war to begin. Don't get me wrong, we don't want the war to start, but we are prepared when it does.

We are God's property, but the enemy doesn't want us to glorify God and live victory-filled lives. Oh, no. He had us in his defeated, death trap once and he makes every attempt to ensnare us again. You can expect it. The sooner you realize that we are at war, and not on a holiday excursion, the more likely you will seek the provisions God has designed for us in the armor pieces. The devil cannot take our souls, now that we have placed our faith in Christ, but he can cause us to live defeated lives… only when we don't appropriate the armor that we've been given to fight with. Let's fight, Ladies! Boot camp is over. You've graduated with honors. You've been given an assignment and the battle is on.

> **Seek the provisions God has designed for us in each of the armor pieces.**

When the battle begins, when the enemy starts shooting arrows of lies, defeat and frustration our way, we must fight back. Besides the truth, righteousness and peace that we spiritually understand and claim as ours, what do we have to fight back with? Our faith. We defend ourselves with our shield of faith.

No Roman soldier would have thought about going into battle without his shield.

There were several different types of shields used by the Roman army, but Paul used the Greek word *thureon* in Ephesians 6:16. This shield was a thick plank of wood measuring 4–4-½ feet by 2-½–3 feet and it provided protection from spears, arrows or fiery darts. It was covered on the outside with metal and sometimes with thick leather. Iron rims were sometimes fitted along the top and bottom edges, and an iron circle was attached to the center of the shield. The boards curved inward and a leather strap was fastened to the back of the shield. Before going into battle, Roman soldiers drenched their leather-covered shields with water. When the fiery arrows of their enemies struck these soaked shields, the flames were immediately extinguished.[1] It was curved to customize and fit around the body and large enough to shield the entire body. Bigger soldier, bigger shield. Petite to plus sizes–but not *one size fits all*. Remember, it's a perfect fit.

The great chapter of faith is Hebrews eleven. The word *faith* is mentioned 23 times of many believers of the Old Testament. It introduces us to men and women of the Old Testament who had spiritual vision and would endure shame and suffering rather than to renounce their faith.

According to Hebrews 11:1, how is faith defined, described and or demonstrated?

Verses 2-3. Who grew in their faith and what evidence is there that we have faith?

God spoke creation into being and we accept that by faith. The world tells us that *seeing is believing,* but God tells us through faith that *believing is seeing.* Faith is very active and full of *doing.* It begins as a seed and continues to grow. In Matthew 17:20, Jesus says, "If you have faith as a mustard seed, you will say to this mountain, 'Move from here to there', and it will move and nothing will be impossible for you."

Many Old Testament men and women of the faith are mentioned in Hebrews 11.

Let's see what we can learn from them.

Hebrews 11:5-6. What was Enoch's testimony?

What do we need to please God?

To you, what does it mean to *diligently seek Him*?

Is your above answer based on faith or works?

 Verse 7. Noah, by faith moved in godly fear. What do you think that means?

As we look at Abraham and Sara's faith (described in Hebrews 11:8-12,17-19) it goes from lesser faith to greater faith. List the five acts of faith, from lesser to greater.

Which acts took more faith? Why?

 Choose one of the great acts of faith mentioned in verses 33-35 and parallel it to a recent example of how you personally saw your faith practiced.

Did that experience cause your faith to strengthen?

These are tremendous victories that valiant soldiers have conquered.

But you may be a weary soldier today, not feeling very valiant, nor victorious. You are rather tired and too exhausted to even pick up your shield. Forget about using it. You may relate more to Hebrews 11:35b-40.

Read those verses and list a few difficulties, *tortures,* which came their way.

They refused to be released because what did they desire? (v. 35)

The world treated them as if they were not worthy to live, but the Word of God exclaims the world was not worthy of them. (Hebrews 11:38) They needed to wait for their victory. But be assured, they received it.

The enemy does shoot arrows at us. Why? We are a threat to him and his kingdom of darkness. When we use our shield of faith to extinguish his arrows, he thinks of other ways to get our focus on fear and ourselves instead of faith in what God promised. The more we use our shield, the better we get at handling it, and the seed of faith begins to grow. In God's power, the *taking* of it becomes automatic and becomes as natural as breathing. When the arrows of doubt, insecurity, worry and fear come our way, we give no thought to them, for our faith far surpasses the struggle.

> **The more we use our shield of faith, the better we get at handling it.**

Understand, it's not *our faith, our abilities, our skills, or our works* that bring the victory; it is the object of our faith–Jesus. He is victorious in our lives. Remember young David's comment to Goliath, "The battle is the Lord's!"

 We grow in our faith as we exercise the shield in the Lord's army. Don't get discouraged if you feel you are not a trained soldier. According to the following verses, how much faith do we need to have the enemy flee?

> **It is not our faith, our abilities, our skills, or our works that bring the victory; it is the object of our faith – Jesus.**

Matthew 21:21   Luke 17:5-6   Romans 12:3-6

And with that size faith what does James 4:7 tell us will happen?

What are you facing today, Soldier Sis? Is your shield of faith in your hand or lying in the corner? _____ (Yes, I'm expecting an answer.) Include this answer in **Sharpen Your Sword for Week Six.** Use one of the faith verses as encouragement.

When we consider the many others that are in the Lord's army with us mentioned Hebrews 11, we can stand encouraged. We are not alone. Hebrews 12:1-2 tells we are to:

#1.) Put down our weight (burden), #2. Run with endurance (wearing our armor) and #3. Look to Jesus (Keep our focus and faith on Him.) He is the author and finisher of our faith. He started it. He will equip us to fight.

 Continue to work on Ephesians 6:10-16. Say "Above all" with conviction!!

The Perfect Fit

Week Six   Day Three

Faith that My Father Knows Best

"Above all, taking the shield of faith, with which you will be able
to quench all the fiery darts of the wicked." Ephesians 6:16

My dad was a boat captain. As a child, I spent many summer days out on the Delaware Bay, on his party boat filled with fishermen ready for a day out and cooler full of fresh fish. Even now, as I think back, I can practically hear the sounds of the seagulls, feel the slime of the squid, and smell the salt in the air and *aroma* of the fish. They are memories I treasure and often wish I could relive, just one more time. When I stroll down Memory Lane, out on the boat, what I remember most is the incredible faith I had in my dad.

Y'see, he was, and is still in my heart, indestructible. I never, not once, doubted our safe return back to shore. Even if the boat were to go down, he would save me. After all, I was his. If the lines got tangled, he would untangle them. (Or at least cut them free.) If I caught a fish that I was not strong enough to reel in, he would take my line, set me straight and then hold me tight while encouraging me to "reel it in". I can see him in my mind standing behind that large wheel, with his muscles bulging, steering the bow of the boat in the right direction. There was never the thought that we might be lost. Never! My dad knew the way. And that always amazed me since out in the middle of the bay, in every direction, it all looks the same—water as far as you can see. But, my dad knew it all, for I never doubted his love and protection over me. Everyone on the boat knew that he would take care of everything. There was no presence of fear. Not a bit!

It was faith I had in him. Unwavering faith. Faith to make life altering decisions for me. Faith to get me safely home. Faith in him to know that he knew which way to turn. He was dad. Of course

> **He sets me straight, holds me tight, and encourages me to trust.**

he knew. A Biblical definition of *faith* is a *belief in and a confident attitude toward God. It involves commitment to His will for one's life.* As I meditate on that definition, I accept that that is the kind of faith that I had in my dad. I surely had a confident attitude toward him, and I agreed that he knew what was best for me. I am still so secure in the love my dad has for me.

Sadly, you might not testify to a similar father-love; and for that, I am sorry. Even though my dad is not a believer in Christ, I believe because of the child-like faith I have in him, it made it easier for me to have such a strong faith in my Lord Jesus. I have <u>no doubts</u> that my God will take care of me. <u>I know</u> He knows what is best for me. Why? Because <u>I am His</u>!

When struggles come my way, He sets me straight, holds me tight, and encourages me to *trust*. He never leaves me alone to *figure it out* on my own. He's my Heavenly Father and I trust Him explicitly. I have faith in Him, there is no room for fear.

 Did you (or do you) have that same faith in your father? If not, is there someone you have that type of faith in?

If you do not, I can understand how fully trusting another can be a challenge. Or maybe you were hurt deeply by someone you did trust fully in. I can relate to that one. Either way, God is perfect and cannot lie. Remember? He is Truth. His promises are true for you and He cares deeply for you.

 According to John 3:16, how deeply does God love you?

I remember many years ago meditating on John 3:16, when my sister and best friend, had a scare with breast cancer. I was walking and chatting with the Lord early one morning when I sensed the Lord ask of me, "Would you be willing to die so that your dad would come to know me?" Without hesitation I responded with a "yes!" That thought didn't need to be considered. If my dying would lead my dad to knowing Jesus as his personal Savior, I was ready to say goodbye to this earth. But then the Lord gently asked me if I would be willing to give up my sister, so that our dad would know Christ. I paused. Actually, I stopped right in my tracks and reflected on that thought for a while. I loved my sister. Her name is written on my heart. I didn't want this cancer to take her life, but I knew that she would feel the same as I did. She loved the Lord **and** our dad. If it were to bring our dad to God's heart, then I knew she would also be ready to say, "Good-bye." I began walking again... a little slower and more purposed than before. Then, <u>THE</u> QUESTION came to my mind and heart. "Would you give up Andrea so that your dad could know me?" I stopped, found a bench, and wept. Andrea was my baby. She was perfect in every way and I loved her more than life itself. The thought of life without her was more than I could imagine. I was speechless, even in my thoughts. Yet, I knew He was waiting for an answer. It was found in John 3:16. There it reads that God loved us so much that

He gave His Son for us. Not only did He sacrifice His perfect, sinless Son; he watched Jesus get beaten, ridiculed, spat upon, and die for sins that He didn't even commit. They were <u>my sins</u> and <u>your sins</u> that broke the heart of our Father and caused His Son to suffer and die.

God was putting the question in my spirit if I would be willing to give up **my** child for someone that I love, my dad. After meditating, weeping, praying and reflecting on God's Word, I answered with a quiet, "yes". I knew that although Andrea was young, she had already trusted Christ as her Savior, her eternal home was secure. In light of eternity, I knew it to be the right answer, but in the day-to-day, the thought caused my heart to physically ache. I pondered why He asked me such a question.

God did not take my sister or my daughter during that time, but did show me that His love is extravagant for me. He loves me THAT much to give me HIS SON. <u>I love my dad so much</u>. Even as I type, tears flow from my eyes at the love I have for him. But God loves Him more. I know that. And, I trust my Father in Heaven to work in my dad's heart to understand the great gift He has given. His love is for my dad. His love is personally yours, also. If you were the only sinner on the planet Earth, He would have sent His Son for you. You can trust Him. You can fully surrender your life to Him. You can and must put all your faith in Jesus Christ for your salvation. Why? For two reasons—*eternal life sake* and *abundant life sake.*

When we place our faith in God, and trust the gift of His Son's death for our sins, eternal life is ours according to John 3:16. Eternal life is a great promise.

According to Romans 3:23-24, how do we secure eternal life?

What happens if we do not trust Christ as our Savior and Lord?

Refer to Psalm 9:17 and Matthew 10:38.

Without faith in Christ, the Bible tells us we are destined for Hell. Eternal life in Heaven is quite a perk of believing. But, we also have many promises of how our life on earth improves as our faith grows. Abundant life is ours according to John 10:10.

Does that mean we will have no struggles or problems? (Answer according to John 16:33)

 Do you have faith that your Father in Heaven will take care of you?

Read Luke 12:4-10. Does this verse encourage or discourage you?

The simple child-like faith that I had in my dad, serves as an example to me of the faith I am encouraged to have in my heavenly Father. My dad loves me, and I am a treasure to him, but my

Father in Heaven loves me even more. I trust Him with my life. He is my shield and He takes care of me, even when the *fiery darts of the wicked* are released. I am His and to my delight, HE IS MINE.

Do you have that same faith in God? Simple, yet complete? It is available to you today. Right now.

 Record any prayer concerns on the **Sharpen Your Sword for Week Six.**

 Add Ephesians 6:16 to the passage that you have been reviewing. I am so proud of your efforts to make Ephesians 6:10-20 part of your everyday life.

The Perfect Fit

Week Six   Day Four

Fiery Darts

"...above all, taking the shield of faith, with which you will be able to quench all the fiery darts of the wicked one." Ephesians 6:16

Thwid! Twang! Thud! Ouch!
This is my attempt at making arrow sounds as they are released from the bow, flying through the air and landing on their target. It's sad, but hopefully you get the idea. They may also sound like this:

Thwid!–You are never going to feel better!

Twang!–No one wants you around anyway!

Thud!–I hate my life!

Ouch!–Nobody cares!

What do the fiery darts of the wicked sound like when they hit you, as the bull's eye? Yes, that right. *You* are the center of the bull's eye!

The enemy aims with great precision at you, as if he were shooting for the bull's eye of a target. I imagine a large target and right in the middle of it is my name. (Of course, in the middle of yours, is YOUR NAME.) And the enemy has had plenty of practice aiming. He's a pretty good shot. He sees my weaknesses and shoots his fiery darts my way. *Thwid! Twang!* Sometimes my bull's eye, the center of my weakness, can be very large–when I'm not walking close to the Lord. And the arrows can hit us at our lowest–*Thud!* And it hurts, because we are out of God's best for us. *Ouch!* Usually when that happens we had not thought of taking up our shield of faith to counter attack.

I know of a woman that has had the *powers of the darkness of this world* shoot arrows at her. She had been ill for many years with *woman problems*. You know, the menstrual ones that we all deal with, but hers were on a very challenging scale. Her bleeding would not stop and it caused much stress on her and her family in many ways. I'm sure she was moody, irritable, had the cramps, headache and backache. She had cleanliness issues, plus she lived in a culture that interpreted her continuous bleeding as unclean and she was treated by many as an outcast. Besides the social and physical problems, financially she had exhausted her funds trying to find a cure. We can read her story in Luke 8. It is a familiar one, but we can gain some application from her about wearing the shield of faith. Let's see what the Spirit can teach us from this woman's plight and her unwavering faith.

The story begins with a leader in the synagogue coming to Jesus because his twelve-year-old daughter was quite ill to the point of death.

Read Luke 8:41-42.
How did Jairus demonstrate his faith?

Oh, how I can relate to going to Jesus over a sick daughter. Have you ever gone to Jesus for healing of a child? Describe the instance that comes to your mind.

Was there any fiery darts that needed to be extinguished?

Here she comes, our woman of the day, (v. 43). According to Luke 8:43-44, what happened?

 This miracle seemed unnoticed and misplaced, but verses 45-46 tell us that someone did notice. And He knew she was in the crowd. Who was it?

I love how this appears to be an *interruption* on the way to a *real* miracle. There are no interruptions, just like there are no coincidences, with God. Long line at the grocery store, sick children, you name it—happenings may *seem* like inconveniences and interruptions, but I believe God orchestrates my day to what is best for me. Yes, poor planning can cause hurried schedules, but shall I say, *sacred interruptions* are what being dressed in the armor of God is all about. Those *divine appointments are* when God comes in and pencils in His will for me today.

What do the following verses say about *my time*?
Psalm 31:15   Psalm 90:12
Ecclesiastes 3:1

Although we can't physically walk on the same road with Jesus, you better believe He knows when we call out to Him in faith. And, we know His will for us when

> **Every time we choose to pick up our shield of faith Heaven notices. Every time.**

we walk in the Spirit with Him. She did not say anything, but her actions demonstrated her faith. There was a lot at risk for her, too. The laws of that time, according to Leviticus 15:25-31 would have made her daily life difficult. She had learned to live with it, let's say endure it, but when Jesus came she knew something was different. Something in her knew she needed to touch Him. She risked public shame. Every time we choose to pick up our shield of faith and use it in the power of Jesus Christ, Heaven notices.

Every time.

She was healed. From where did her healing come? (v. 47)

Let's finish the biblical account of this story. Read Luke 8:47-48.

How would you describe her emotional state? Was she confident? Fearful? Bold? Humble?

   What endearing term does Christ call her?

I love that! I believe it is the only recorded time in scripture that Jesus referred to someone with that term. Imagine, we are soldiers in the army, but daughters of the King. Both define who we truly are as we walk in His will for our lives.

What healed her? (Be careful here) Refer to 8:48
What do you imagine her shield of faith looked like?

Twelve years of flaming arrows! We know this was a physical condition, but the enemy had to have had a field day crushing her spirit emotionally. Day after day. Lie after lie. Defeat after defeat. If she had faith in the beginning, I'm sure it was a bit weak at this point. Perhaps you have a long-term trial that appears God has not noticed. You've possibly taken it to Him so many times that there seems no point anymore. It might be a bad marriage, an unfaithful husband, a wayward child, a physical condition, a hurtful *friend,* a difficult relative- you fill in the blank. There is no peace and no end in sight from your perspective.
Trust me, Friend. God knows. He sees. And He cares for you, Daughter.

You may have lifted your shield of faith about this issue so many times that your arms are tired. You've put it down and have now settled for arrows of darkness to strike you and even stick. You're down. Hurting. This is the life you've settled on. Is this the life you want?

Rate your faith level about the situation that came to mind … Place a mark somewhere between:

Victimized—— Victorious
(By countless arrows)   (By use of your shield)

Sometimes arrows hit us and, because of their sharp, angled points, they cannot be pulled out at the location they entered. Once the arrow penetrates the skin deep enough the only way to remove it is to work it through to the other side. It would actually cause more damage to try and reverse it at the entry point. All that can be done is to either cut it out or work it through. Difficulties, trials and temptations are that way, too. Sometimes when we surrender to them and choose to not be dressed in the full armor of God, we must allow them to play out with all their horrible effects. We do reap what we sow and the consequences of our actions are painful. Some alter our lives, some we must simply survive, and others we must learn from as we *work it through*.

God can take our failures—those moments when we have been defeated by the enemy's arrows—and turn them into victories. Even though we must reap the consequences of our poor choices, we can be victorious in knowing that we picked up our shield of faith and chose to believe God. He picks up the pieces and works the miraculous. She had issues! The scriptures refer to her problems as an issue of blood, but current vernacular uses the term *issues* in other ways. Any personality, emotional, social or inter-relational problem you have can be called an *issue*. I overheard my daughter describe an impatient mom as having *issues*. She had no physical conditions, but emotionally she was not being controlled by the Holy Spirit. She had issues. You have issues. I do, too.

Faith is the basis for all victories in the conflicts and triumphs of the life. What do the following verses remind you of concerning placing your trust and faith in God?

Psalm 37:3   Psalm 115:9-13

He is my help and shield. When the arrows fly my way in the midst of my conflicts, God has a counter *shield-move* to defeat them. Below are a several different arrows that might fly at you in a normal day. Besides the whispered lies of the enemy, the darkness of this world has other tactics to make us think we are defeated. He knows we are lazy and often do not pick up the shield of faith. In the left column are the fiery darts of the wicked one. On the right is the way we are taught, according to God's principles, to appropriate the shield of faith. Following God's way is a verse to support its teaching. Try to match them. (They are not in order.):

FIERY DARTS BRING:	THE SHIELD OF FAITH BRINGS:
Fear	Confidence and Strength (Deut. 1:8)
Discouragement	Contentment (Philippians 2:14)
Condemning others	Love or Faith (1 John 4:18)
Complaining	Songs of Praise (Ephesians 5:19-20)
Gossip	Putting Up With Others (Col. 3:12-13)
Regret and Shame	Confidentiality (Proverbs 20:19)
Self-pity	God's Forgiveness (Acts 3:19)
Worry	God First (Matthew 6:33)
Sexual immorality	Patience (2 Timothy 2:24)
Being rude	Rest (Matthew 11:28-29)
Anger	Sexual fidelity (1 Thes. 4:3)
Me First	Being considerate (Titus 3:2)

Circle three of the above arrows that have been aimed at you in the past couple of days. *Talk about issues!!! Let's talk louder of victory!*

What happened to the *woman with the issue* after she was healed? Check out Luke 8:48.

"Daughter"–An expression of endearment from your Father.

"Be of good cheer."–We can receive this encouragement, when we are Spirit filled.

"Your faith has made you well."–We can only hear the Lord say that to us after we have appropriated our shield.

"Go in peace."–Walking in the peace of God is victorious living.

 Out of those four saying of Jesus, which means to most to you today? Why?

(Oh, Happy Day! You have the right to choose all four.)

Hold up our shield of faith and listen carefully as your Heavenly Father says to you,
"Daughter, Be of good cheer.
Your faith has made you well.
Go in peace."

Fill in any requests on the **Sharpen Your Swords for Week Six**. Be sure to write a corresponding scripture verse.

 Continue to memorize Ephesians 6:10-16.

The Perfect Fit

Week Six   Day Five

My Shield of Faith

"Above all, taking the shield of faith, where with ye shall be able to quench all the fiery darts of the wicked." Ephesians 6:16

Yesterday, we left Jairus with a heavy heart, on his knees pleading with Jesus, amidst a multitude of believers. He was a leader in the synagogue and was accustomed to being heard, but when he was in the crowd, as recorded in Luke eight, he was a dad broken-hearted over his daughter's illness. Can you imagine his thought process as he stood waiting for Jesus to converse with the woman? She received healing because of her great faith, but the timing had to have been interpreted as an interruption, maybe even an irritation. Every minute counted—it was truly a matter of the life and death of his precious twelve-year-old daughter.

I can relate a bit to Jairus' heartache. I'll never forget a dreary, early December morning, a few years ago, when we got the call that my father-in-law had taken a turn for the worse. He had been in a Philadelphia hospital with cancer. We were there the day before, but didn't realize the end was to be so soon. As quickly as we could make arrangements for our daughters to get to school, we were in the car, and on the way, amidst the morning rush hour. As we sat in traffic on a crowded highway, my husband phoned his aunt who was already at the hospital. At that moment, she informed him of Dad's passing. My husband let out a deep moan and then we sat in silence. He so wanted to *be there*. He had missed his mom's passing a few months earlier and was determined to be with his dad. This was not just his Dad, but his mentor and best friend. I remember looking through my tears at the other cars around us. Our lives were changed forever, never to be the same. Our hearts were broken to our very souls, yet everyone around was listening to music, sipping coffee, talking on the phone—just on their daily morning commute. I just wanted the traffic jam to part like the Red Sea, but I knew it would not. It was surreal. Our broken hearts just had to wait... just like Jairus'.

As Jesus speaks this healing phrase to the woman, "Daughter, be of good cheer, your faith has made you well. Go in peace." Jairus waits for Jesus to take notice of him.

Read Luke 8:49. What happened while he waited?

When Jairus came in the beginning, he knew that Jesus could heal his sick daughter. He was wearing his shield of faith and ready to quench all the fiery darts of the wicked one. How do you think he feels now?

I'm reading between the lines, but I want to put some flesh onto Jairus. A couple of things could have happened at this point. He could have been so discouraged by the words of the messenger, he put his shield of faith down. We could understand if he did, but know that it would be opening himself to being struck by those fiery darts. Or, his faith could have been strengthened by seeing the miracle of the woman. We don't know. But we do know what Jesus says to him in verse 50. What would you determine was Jairus' faith level at this point?

"Don't be afraid." For Jesus to have said that, there must have been some fear in this man's heart. Let's be real, he was just told his daughter had died! His shield, as well as his hope, was put aside. But Jesus tells him to "Don't be afraid." I would love to spend the entire study today looking at the phrase, "Don't be afraid", but we have other matters to cover. But, do you realize that fear-not phrases are mentioned in the Bible 366 times? That is one for every day of the year and one to spare! God tells us repeatedly to be fearless. Here, Jesus says it to Jairus.

The *replacement principle* is set into motion here. Jesus tells Jairus to not _____ , but to _____. By obeying in faith, and not being afraid, you are picking up your shield.

 Is there currently a situation in *your* life that Jesus is telling you directly to "Fear not!"?

"Only believe", Jesus told Jairus. And he tells us to only believe Him daily. By believing in faith, you are picking up your shield.

Read Luke 8:51-53. Make a list of all the people involved in this story.

Besides the ones we can name, there were many, actually multitudes in the town, and outside their home. I imagine a friend or two traveled with Jairus to find Jesus. Many stayed back at the house with Mrs. Jairus and the others. In a group that size, do you think there were any believers? Why?

Do you believe that our faith is affected by the faith of those surrounding us?

My personal faith is strengthened by those faithful ones around me. I am blessed to have a multitude of friends and family that are believers in Christ. I have the opportunity to pray for them, and they for me. I am privileged to be a part of a local Bible-believing church that challenges me to grow, worships corporately, and makes me accountable to participate in the body of Christ. One of my greatest joys, within the church, is that I currently teach a Ladies Sunday School class. We have an intimate bond, a *Sisterhood* that is such a gift to me. We share our hearts and lives with one another. They inspire me in more ways than they'll ever know. When my faith is weakened by fear, doubt, or discouragement, they are there for me. They, and others I am blessed to walk this earth, are like the *tortoise formation* used by Roman soldiers of Paul's day. The Roman military worked together using a formation known as the *tortoise*. In the tortoise, the rows of soldiers closed all gaps between one another and held their shields at the edges. The first row of men placed their shields in from of them to protect the formation's front; soldiers on the flanks held their shields to the side. The troops in the middle balanced their shields on their helmets and overlapped them, protecting the formation from above. The formation protected the soldiers like a shell protects a tortoise. As long as the soldiers remained together in this formation, they were nearly undefeatable.[1]

The shield described by Paul was intended to be used in company with others, and so is our faith. How are we to lean on and learn from sisters and brothers in the faith?

Galatians 6:2	Ecclesiastes 4:12	1 Peter 2:17
1 John 1:7	Romans 12:10	

The local church or *body of Christ* or *fellowship of believers* is so important to help us develop the way we use our shield of faith. I can recall more than one time when a sister has helped me hold my shield, when I was too weary to lift my arms. Corporate worship is also necessary to our growing faith. I believe that Jairus was encouraged in his faith by his friends.

When Jesus got to Jairus' home, what happened in Luke 8:51-53?

What did that say? Some *ridiculed* Jesus? What?! Read that to me again.

Jesus, the Son of God, was standing right there. He had made a house call to heal a child. And, yet, there were those in the crowd that ridiculed Him. They *knew* she was dead. Jesus is there, faithful friends are there, and a miracle is about to take place. And the enemy is there also ridiculing our faith. I'm sure we can all think of a sister or brother in the faith that *know* our circumstances and seem to take our shield of faith right out of our hands. I swallow hard to say this, but I'm sure I have been confident about something, spoke my mind, only later to realize my comments could have hurt someone's faith. My heart breaks at the thought.

In the Greek this is translated, "they laughed Him to scorn". Can you imagine it?

Is Jesus affected by their ridicule?
Not a chance. He was not distracted for a moment. What happened in Luke 8:54-46?

Jesus put them outside, separated the Jairus family from those that discouraged their faith. We also need to *separate ourselves* from the crowd and be alone with the Lord, especially when we are weary. When we keep our eyes on Him and under teaching that strengthens our faith—we hear HIS VOICE. Miracles happen. Our faith grows. Brothers and sisters of the faith stand next to us and intercede for us in prayer, but our confidence is in Jesus. Remember Hebrews 12:1-2, HE is the author and finisher of our faith. When we hold our shield of faith firmly in place, heed his commands, the fiery darts cannot touch us.

Like in verse 54, He also *takes us by the hand* and says to us, "Little girl, arise!" When I have my shield of faith in my hand I arise in obedience. I may have been discouraged by situations and people, but when I listen to Jesus my strength and faith return. I think all of us women have a *little girl* inside us that needs to be sheltered and loved. We each have a *little girl* that needs to be taken by the hand, encouraged, and heard.

Who are some people that you have tried to have meet the needs of that *little girl* within?

 In reference to this story of Jairus' daughter, who is the only One who can give us life? According to verse 55, what happened within her?

When we are discouraged, Little Girls, we need our spirit to return. When your spirit returns, your faith is renewed and your shield is strong and you are ready to let the Lord battle for you. Luke 8:56 says her parents were astonished. If you used your shield of faith the way it was purposed to be used, do you think others would be astonished? Would you be?

So, Sister Soldier, what does your shield of faith look like? Mine is similar to a Roman soldiers and protects my entire body from the enemy. It's pure white, light-weight, and covered with the water of the Spirit. In the center is a large red cross to remind me that it is not *my* faith that matters, but **who** my faith is in. It is my personal faith in Jesus Christ that has given my faith the victory.

Does my shield of faith have dings and dents in it? You better believe it. It appears to be pretty banged up. Each mark represents a victory that my faith has won. Every dent is a reminder that the enemy has no place to discourage, distract or defeat me. I use my shield of faith to be valiant in the daily battles sent my way. I use it on behalf of my sisters and brothers. My faith cannot be their faith, but I can encourage them by holding my shield high, standing beside them in tortoise formation and fighting for them in prayer. And, I can humble myself and be strengthened by them when my arms get tired.

Little Girl, Arise. Let your spirit return. He's reaching out to you.
Take Him by the hand. And with the other, hold your shield of faith high.
He promises to astonish you!!!

Write any prayer concerns on **Sharpen Your Swords for Week Six**. Perhaps a verse from our story of Jairus would be a perfect companion.

Recite Ephesians 6:10-16.

The Perfect Fit

Sharpen Your Sword

Week Five

Concern	Truth to Believe	Date	Answer
A worry	Proverbs 3:5-6 "He will direct my paths."		

The Perfect Fit

Week Six Wrap Up

Principal Questions for Week Six

1. What are we to do *above all* in the following verses? Which is your priority?

1 Chronicles 16:25 _____

Colossians 3:14 _____

Ephesians 6:16 _____

2. List the five acts of faith in Hebrews 11:8-12, 17-19, from lesser to greater.

3. According to John 3:16, how deeply does God love you?

4. Where did the woman with the issue of blood (Luke 8:47) healing come from?

5. According to Luke 8:55,56, what happened within Jarius' daughter

Practical Questions for Week Six

1. How do the truths in Deuteronomy 7: 14 and Exodus 19:5 make you feel?

2. Think about the great acts of faith in verses Hebrews 11:33-35; which have you seen in your life lately?

3. Is there a person in your life who helped you develop your faith in God as the Heavenly Father?

4. What do you imagine the woman with the issue of blood's shield of faith looked like?

5. Is there a situation in *your* life that Jesus is telling you directly to "Fear not!"?

The Perfect Fit

Session Seven – Helmet of Salvation

"And take the helmet of salvation" Ephesians 6:17a

Is. 59:17   Eph. 1:13   I Thes. 5:8   Matt 5:11-12   I John 1:9   Proverbs 23:7 2   Tim1:12

The helmet of the Roman soldier would protect his skull and neck from enemy's weapons. It was well-made, and specifically designed. The helmet was strong, fashioned from bronze or iron. The officer's helmet often had a crest with a dyed plume of horse's hair a top.

Protection for the _____. **Thinking on God's Word is necessary in our daily lives.**

For the weapons of our warfare are not of the flesh but have divine power to destroy strongholds. We destroy arguments and every *lofty opinion* raised against the knowledge of God, and take *every thought* captive to obey Christ, being ready to punish every disobedience, when your obedience is complete. 2 Cor. 10:4-6

1. A daily _____. Think on these things. Phil 4:8

> Finally, sisters, whatever is true, whatever is honorable, whatever is just, whatever is pure, Whatever is lovely, whatever is commendable, if there is any excellence? If there is anything worthy of praise, think about these things.

2. The _____ begins here, but not _____ here.
3. We are to take God's wisdom.

Have the _____ of _____. Phil 2:5 Jesus is our salvation.

What we "have"–_____, _____, and _____.

What we "take"–_____, _____, and _____.

"Then all the assembly shall know that the Lord does not save with sword and spears,

For the battle is the Lord's, and He will give you into our hands." I Sam 17:47

The Perfect Fit

Week Seven   Day One

The Helmet of Salvation

"And take the helmet of salvation…" Ephesians 6:17

While vacationing last summer, I witnessed a horrible bicycle accident. I was sitting outside my room very late at night, chatting with some friends, when a sweet young staff worker missed a turn and found herself face first in the street. We rushed over to assist and found she was in dire need of medical assistance and prayer. The professionals came, prayers were raised to the heavens and several surgeries later, she is doing well. All glory to God for this miracle!! (As a matter of fact, I just saw her this year at the same vacation spot and she still has two surgeries to go.) We know that God allows all things for a reason, but much of this particular pain and suffering could have possibly been avoided, if only she had been wearing a helmet.

I'm sure you could share a *bike helmet* story of your own. We know the importance of wearing them, but many of us believe we are exempt from accidents. My husband is quite the cyclist and he is an advocate for the advantages of wearing a helmet. Just ask him. He is faithful to wear his even if he is only going around the block. He's out there on the streets and realizes the reality of falling. The true cyclist knows the importance of wearing a bike helmet and the follower of Christ, that desires to live the promised abundant life, knows she needs the helmet of salvation.

The Roman soldier's armor that Paul references in Ephesians includes a helmet. Ours is called the *helmet of salvation*. The Romans had the best helmet of the ancient world. Some possessed a chin-strap, visor, and came down to cover the back and sides of the neck. It had a lining of leather, sponge or felt and therefore was softened for comfort and a good fit. The helmet was made of bronze for the soldiers, iron alloy for officers, and others were made of medal. The highest-ranking officers had gold and silver alloy helmets for parade dress. It was the most noticeable piece of armor. It was often ornate, intricately decorated and plumed with brightly dyed feathers or horsehair. Some parade dress helmets had course horsehair plumes that would extend to the waist. This helmet was designed so that blows from sword, hammer or ax could not pierce it but would be deflected and yet allow the soldier maximum visibility.[1]

When we hear the term *salvation* we immediately think of the initial salvation needed from sin. This helmet of salvation *does not* refer to that moment we ask Christ to be our Savior. The book of Ephesians was written for believers and this full armor passage was for believers engaged in warfare. You are not even in the army unless you are a believer. If you're not, Satan has no interest in you for you are already his property.

The *helmet of salvation* is more than the assurance of salvation—although the knowledge we are saved is included in what is meant. It is the *beginning* of our salvation. It is the *past* of the tenses of salvation. The scriptures teach us that we <u>are</u> saved (saving us from the penalty of sin)—PAST, that we <u>are being</u> saved (saving us from the power of sin)—PRESENT, and that we <u>shall be</u> saved (saving us from the presence of sin)—FUTURE.[2]

 Read the three verses below and place beside each, one of the following words: PAST, PRESENT, or FUTURE.

_____ 2 Corinthians 1:10

_____ Romans 5:10

_____ Ephesians 2:8

Salvation touches the past, present and future of our Christian lives and is important to understand the *helmet of salvation,* so we can appropriate it as a part of our everyday attire.

The phrase *helmet of salvation* is also mentioned in Isaiah 59:17a, as well as Ephesians 6:17. *For He put on righteousness as a breastplate, and a helmet of salvation on His head.*

Isaiah is known as the *little Bible* because it carries some similarities:

The Bible has 66 books, 39 Old Testament and 27 New Testament. Isaiah has 66 chapters, 39 about Law—Government of God and 27 on Grace—Salvation of God. Isaiah is a book of prophecy and the first of the Prophetic books. It is also known as the fifth gospel. In it we read of Christ's virgin birth, His character, His life, His death, His resurrection and His second coming. In the middle of the section on grace, and the salvation that God provides, is Isaiah 59.

 Read Isaiah 59:1-3. Why are we separated from God?

 Have you ever felt like God was far away? Who moved? God or us? _____

In Isaiah 59:3-8, God spells out some of the iniquities or sin we commit. In Isaiah 59:9-19, the sin is confessed in specifics. Isaiah 59:15b-19 we see the salvation of the Lord on our behalf.

He forgave their sin and brought "a helmet of salvation on His head". We praise Him because as sin abounds, so does God's grace, mercy and forgiveness.

Have you confessed specific sin today?

Are you clean before the Lord?

Do you actually feel the burdens lifted?

If so, with a heart full of praise and thanksgiving, list a few blessings that God has bestowed upon you from verses 16-20.

 Record your confession of sin in **Sharpen Your Sword for Week Seven**. Write verse.

The Redeemer has come! His name is Jesus. He put righteousness on as a breastplate. God put the helmet of salvation onto Jesus' head. He is our helmet.

How carefully did you read verse 19? Did you catch the INCREDIBLE blessing at the end of the verse? (I'm so excited, I can barely type.)

When the enemy comes in like a flood,
The Spirit of the LORD will lift up a standard against him.

Last week we discussed *taking* as opposed to *having* the armor. Please list the three pieces you *have*:

_____ _____ _____

Now list the three pieces you *take*: _____ _____ _____

Understand, if we *take* something from someone, we *receive it.*

So go ahead, humbly receive the helmet of salvation from the hand of the Lord. The promise is that Jesus is our helmet of salvation. He saved us in the past from our penalty of sin, continually cleanses us presently from the power of sin, and will be our salvation for future sin. It is His helmet that we receive – and someday we will cast it at His feet. *His hand is not short that He cannot save* (Isaiah 59:1). Reach out and receive the helmet, confessing sin and rejoicing in the Redeemer that has been sent for us today.

 Add Ephesians 6:17 to the end of Ephesians 6:10-16. (It is the shortest addition, only six words.) Keep reviewing from verse 10 to 17a. You can do this!!

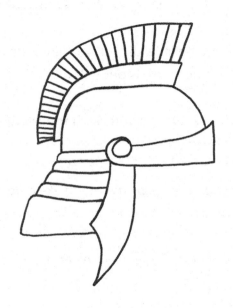

The Perfect Fit

Week Seven   Day Two

Just a Li'l bit of Brownies

"And take the helmet of salvation…" Ephesians 6:17

I don't like chocolate. It doesn't really *do* anything for me. I rarely find myself craving it and I have no problem passing it by on a dessert tray. I realize that many of you reading this may now be convinced I am thoroughly crazy and have lost my mind. You may even find me heretical! Occasionally, you *will* find me baking brownies. I can live without them, but my Samantha loves chocolate and brownies are her favorite.

My brownie recipe is a little different than most. I buy whatever brownie box mix is on sale, add the eggs, milk, water, butter and other ingredients, mix them until smooth and then I add one level teaspoon of dog poop. (Yes, that is not a misprint… I said *dog poop*.) It adds a special texture, a certain aroma and an irresistibly indescribable flavor. Once people find out about my recipe they tend to not desire my brownies. They taste good, but it's something about the ingredients that turns their stomachs. It's only a teaspoon in an entire batch—I just don't get the reactions. If I didn't tell, no one would know. I mean, what's the difference? You go to church, listen, and learn how to apply God's Word. Through the week you even read your Bible and pray. You listen to Christian music and, on occasion, even share your faith. You don't use profane language, cheat on your husband, or chew tobacco. In all honesty, you are a pretty good Christian woman.

So what! You very occasionally watch a movie with profanity, casual sex or worldly values. *No big deal!* You talk about others when they are not there. (And you say things you would not say to their faces. Be honest here.) *You're just being a friend* when you choose to be a *sounding board* when others are talking about others. It's a *fine line*. It's really *not your fault* that you lose your cool often with your husband or children. And *you're not really **doing** anything wrong* when you entertain inappropriate thoughts

> **Spiritual warfare is going to be won or lost in the mind.**

about others. All of this is as innocent as the *little bit* of dog poop that I put in my brownie recipe. It's just a *tiny bit*. Don't you agree?

Just as the Roman soldier's helmet protected his head from injury, so the helmet of salvation must protect our minds from wicked thoughts, which lead to wicked actions, which lead to wicked habits. In many respects, spiritual warfare is going to be won or lost in the mind, and it matters VERY MUCH what we fill it with. You can be sure that if Satan defeats a believer it will be through their mind. Many a spiritual battle is fought in the mind... with just a little bit of *dog poop*.

I know you deal with this stuff, because I do. We live in a real world filled with evil, filth, and unholy opportunities at every turn. As believers, we also live in a spiritual world where the *rulers of the darkness of this age* are active and out to defeat us. We can blame our surroundings, situations, circumstances, husbands, financial status, children, and/or jobs, but even if we lived in a *perfect world*, Satan and his *wickedness in high places* would find a way to get into our thought-life. Remember Eve? She lived in the perfect world, had the perfect man, and walked with God. She had no dishes to do, laundry to keep up, shopping to squeeze in or children to mind. And yet, Satan found her at her weakest point; he messed with her mind.

Let's go back to the beginning with Eve. You remember the setting. God has just created his beautiful universe by merely speaking it into being, and then decided to create man "in His own image, male and female he created them, Genesis 1:27." He breathed life into Adam, and created Eve from Adam's rib and set them in a perfect garden where all their needs would be met. And even there, Satan found Eve and tempted her.

Read Genesis 3:1-5. The serpent came and questioned God's authority and His Word. Adam and Eve were created innocent, but not righteous and therefore fell. According to J. Vernon McGee, *"Righteousness is innocence that has been maintained in the presence of temptation. Temptation will either develop you or destroy you. It will do one of the two. Character must be developed, and it can only be developed in the presence of temptation."*

Temptation came to the innocent Eve, and she fell for it. She was not wearing the full armor of God and the fiery arrows struck and destroyed. Think like a woman. What about Satan's question was *tempting* for her?

 Before she took of the fruit of the forbidden tree, what do you think went through her mind?

Satan's question cast doubt on the words of God. He raised a doubt in her mind about the validity of God's very words. Have you ever doubted God's promises?

> **Satan found her at her weakest point; he messed with her mind.**

Here are just a few promises. Place a check besides the ones you have doubted.

_____ 2 Peter 3:9 *"The Lord is not slack concerning his promise, as some men count slackness; but is longsuffering to us."* Have you ever doubted God's timing?

_____ Hebrews 13:6 *"So that we may boldly say, 'The Lord is my helper, and I will not fear what man shall do unto me.'"* Have you ever doubted the fact that you didn't have to fear man? Ever get anxious over it?

_____ Ephesians 4:32 *"And be ye kind one to another, tenderhearted, forgiving one another, even as God for Christ's sake hath forgiven you."* Have you ever doubted this to be possible? Does it seem impossible for you to be kind and forgiving to a certain individual? Have you ever thought that they didn't deserve your forgiveness?

_____ *Proverbs 22:6 "Train up a child in the way he should go, and when he is old he will not depart from it."* While training your child, have you ever doubted the validity of this verse? Or you knew of some great parents that have a wayward child and doubt this promise was meant for them? Oh, I have.

Do you doubt the Word of God? Just a Li'l bit?

There have been times my words have spoken belief, and maybe even my actions, but my *thoughts* have been different. I have entertained *a li'l bit of doubt* by allowing Satan's arrows to pierce my thinking. I looked with my eyes instead of my faith. And so did Eve. It is even confirmed in the New Testament.

What does 2 Corinthians 11:3 say was Eve's downfall?

Decided *doubt* always leads to disobedience. Read Genesis 3:6-7 and see what I mean.

List three *things* Eve saw and what was going through her mind? (v. 6)

#1. _____ (Appeal to her flesh)

#2. _____ (Appeal to her flesh and mind)

#3. _____ (Appeal to religious side of man)

She did some serious thinking before she ate. She thought it through completely. Wouldn't you know the first thought, first temptation to a woman was about food. Does Satan know our weakness or what? I'm not talking about over-indulging on chocolates – it was a piece of fruit. But it was still disobedience. When the seed of doubt is placed in our mind by the enemy, THIS IS THE MOMENT that we need to *take the helmet of salvation*.

Our mind is where the battle begins. The decision to go to war or surrender to the enemy is made right there. Whatever is in the mind determines behavior and the things that are in our minds are the raw materials from which our entire lives are molded. Satan just wants a foot in the door of our minds to mold our thinking. Just a little bit... a level teaspoon of dog poop.

Record any prayer requests in the **Sharpen Your Sword for Week Seven**. Include a promise of God that you know you cannot doubt.

Start from the top of Ephesians 6:10 ... how far were you able to recite?

The Perfect Fit

Week Seven   Day Three

A Choice to Embrace

"And take the helmet of salvation..." Ephesians 6:17

*L*ife isn't easy. Troubles, pain, heartache, tears and sadness are real and none of us are exempt. But I don't have to tell you that. I'm sure you could make a list of difficulties of your own. Me, too. All of them are not arrows sent from the enemy, but each of them *is* an opportunity to grow in our faith, build our character and more expertly appropriate our armor. So how does wearing our helmet of salvation better equip us to handle the day-to-day troubles that life brings our way? I'm so glad you asked.

It all begins with making a choice to *accept* the challenging seasons of life. It's a CHOICE and when our mind and thought-process is covered with the helmet of salvation, it is a God-ward choice. We can *react* to trials or we can *respond* Biblically. The first step is to accept that troubles will come, to know that God is not surprised for an instant, and that He is present.

James 1:2-3 says to "Count it all joy when we fall into trials of many kinds." Does that mean we ENJOY the trials? The *joy* comes in knowing that God is at work, and being in His presence, not working through the trial. (Psalm 16:11) When trials come we can fight their existence or accept them in our lives. We *react* or *respond.* I suggest we *accept,* then *respond.*

How would you interpret 2 Corinthians 13:7-10 in the light of our response to our trials and troubles?

God will not allow anything to come our way that His power alive in us cannot handle.

Let's consider John 15:1-11. This passage reminds us to *abide* in the Lord. When we abide in Him, we are dressed in the armor that is designed for us. Our mind is Christ-centered because our helmet is securely fastened. According to John 15:1-11, why did Jesus say these things to us?

If we don't ENJOY troubles, do we ENDURE them?

Enduring something does not sound pleasant. No joy there!! When I think of enduring, I think of a recent day at an amusement park. I usually enjoy most roller coasters, log flumes, Ferris-wheels, the works. I'm usually okay with any of them. I scream for fun and have a blast, but while chaperoning on a class trip there was a little girl in my group that wanted to ride and no friend was willing to ride with her. So, I volunteered. No big deal! We got in this cage-looking device, strapped in and off we went. About 15 seconds into this one, I knew I wanted off. It jerked, banged, whipped and was not fun at all. I prayed and ENDURED the rest of the ride. Maybe I'm getting too old for these things.☺

God does not want us to endure trials long-faced. There is no trusting in that; He wants us to lean on Him for our every need. The epistle of 2 Timothy, written also by Paul, speaks much about enduring.

Read the following verses and write what is to be *endured* and why.

2 Timothy 2:3 _____

2 Timothy 2:8-13_____

2 Timothy 4:1-5 _____

In contrast, note what Psalms states about God's character and enduring.

Psalm 16:3-4 _____

Psalm 100:5 _____

Psalm 112:3 _____

Psalm 119:90 _____

> **He endures and is alive in us. Therefore, we can endure with great victory.**

He endures and is alive in us, therefore we can endure with great victory.

> **God is more concerned with our character,**
>
> **than with our circumstance.**

I believe God's desire is for us to EMBRACE troubles and tribulations. We cannot realistically ENJOY them; should not with a long face ENDURE them; but we are able to EMBRACE what God has for us in them. I love the word *embrace*.

I'm a hugger, so the word *embrace* is flooded with peace, joy and contentment to me. Think of a warm embrace with a trusted friend. Or the simple embrace of a loving child. We can embrace people, but also ideas and seasons of life.

What are we to *embrace* in Proverbs 4:5-9?

When are we to *embrace* according to Ecclesiastes 3:5?

Webster defines *embrace* as to *clasp in the arms or to accept readily*. While wearing our helmet of salvation, we are intentionally deciding to embrace the difficult situations in which we find ourselves. Embracing them is accepting from God what He chooses to bring our way, and trusting Him to build our faith and Christian character. God is more concerned with our character than our circumstance.

Don't get me wrong; some difficult places we find ourselves in the middle of are self-induced. When we lose our temper with a friend and speak out of turn, the strain on the relationship was not permitted by God, but produced by our selfishness. We cannot enjoy, endure or even embrace it, we must ask for forgiveness and attempt reconciliation. I'm sure you could think of a similar situation. The beautiful thing is, even in a self-induced tribulation, we can surrender to God and in obedience respond in the way He would have us. Usually, it is overflowing with His love and possibly some humble pie. (And humility is a great quality.)

So, if more tribulations produce a deeper walk with the Lord, then I would have to say, "Bring it on!" I passionately want to know Him more and more. It is in the midst of them that I am most needy of His guidance. It is then that I find myself at His feet, seeking His leading. At His feet is my favorite place to be.

 It is a decision of the will how we will handle what God allows to come into our lives. It is not normal to embrace difficulties. It is so opposite the world's standards and expectations. Remember, every time we make a move toward God, the enemy makes a move toward us. Look at 2 Corinthians 10:3-6. What does verse 3 say we *do not* war against?
What is *that* according to Romans 7:18?

This fact does not surprise us at this point in the study. We war against the enemies and our flesh. According to 2 Corinthians 10:4, what weapons do we use to fight? Give some detail.

 What two things are we to do (look for verbs) to aid in obedience to Christ?

Every thought to the obedience of Christ. Every single thought! We put on the helmet that we have been given, make a clear decision that we choose to embrace God's will, and are ready to fight the enemy. The enemy plays dirty and whispers in our ears unkind thoughts of others, defeated thoughts of ourselves, or creates worry and fear. It is then we say, "Get thee behind me Satan," sharpen a sword, and focus on embracing God's power.

Troubles come. How do we handle them? Do we enjoy? Endure? React? Respond? Complain? Accept? Embrace with grace?

WOW! You never know what God has planned.

Are you in the midst of a trial and cannot quite make sense of God's purpose in it?

He sees the bigger picture. He knows how *the story* and *our story* ends. Trust Him. His love will endure for you. He will bring joy and peace when our mind is stayed on Him. Put on your helmet of salvation and choose to embrace His plan for you.

 Sharpen your sword today by choosing a verse from today's study that would help you embrace a trial that you are currently walking through. Record in **Sharpen Your Sword for Week Seven.**

 Recite Ephesians 6:10-17 to someone today.

The Perfect Fit

Week Seven   Day Four

Marching Orders

"And take the helmet of salvation..." Ephesians 6:17

*O*kay, Soldier Sis! You have on your belt of truth to know that He is the Truth. You have put on your breastplate of righteousness and shoes of peace. You have received from the Commander-in-Chief your shield of faith and helmet of salvation. All pieces fit perfectly and you are ready to defend yourself from the enemy. You are dressed. You have no weapon as of yet, but ready for your *marching orders* for the day. Picture yourself in a military lineup – dressed, ready to go, listening to your Authority.

"Attention!"

"About Face!"

"Forward March!"

We are given some marching orders to follow in 1 Thessalonians, mainly to encourage our fellow soldiers with the *hope of our salvation*, which we are to wear as a helmet. Let's begin by reading 1 Thessalonians 5:1-5. One of the reasons Paul was writing to the Thessalonians was because there was some misunderstanding with regard to future end-time events. He wrote to encourage, clarify and correct them.

When is the day of the Lord to come?

I love the surprise effect comparing to labor pains. Many of us could write a novel on those, could we not? And what about that line, "and they shall not escape"? Think back to those labor pains, there was no escaping. But the end result was definitely worth the effort–that sweet precious one in your arms.

Are we as believers to be surprised? (v. 4)

What are believers called in verse 5?

Okay, Soldiers of the Light! The marching orders are to begin. There are many, so let's number them as we go to keep them in order. The first three in 1 Thessalonians 5:6.

#1. _____ #2. _____ #3. _____

Read verses 7–8. More orders are given.

Record the two mentioned in verse 8. #4. _____ (sounds familiar) and #5. _____ (Bingo! The featured armor of the week).

This is the third and final time in Scripture that the helmet of salvation is mentioned and the first time it is associated with the *hope of salvation*. Let's look at 1 Thessalonians 5:8 a little bit closer. According to Calvin, "Faith alone saves, but the faith that saves is not alone." "Faith" looks to the past when we accepted the Lord Jesus Christ. "Love" is for the present, which is the relationship the believer should have with those around him. The "hope of salvation" is that blessed hope of the future. It is the consummation of our salvation. When we see Christ our salvation will be complete.

1 Thessalonians 5:9 gives us the most important marching order, actually, we need it to be recruited into the army. What is it?

I was 7 years old when, at a gospel concert, I went forward to accept Christ as my Savior. I had been raised in church and knew of this blessed salvation, but I personalized it on that day. I realized "I" was a sinner and needed forgiveness. I don't recall a tremendous change in my life at that moment. As I grew into my teen years I was, by the world's standard a *good* girl, but I justified my sin constantly. Anyone looking on would have thought I was an ideal young Christian woman, but God knew the depths of my hypocrisy. At 19, while randomly visiting a Wednesday night Bible study at a local church, I heard a message on Heaven. One of the verses used was Revelation 22:4-5. "They shall see His face." I'll never forget the moment.

I Thes 5:10 – I am to (#6) _____ Live with Him. #7. Comfort each other.

My sin was made real to me, and I had the awakening that I was going to see Jesus and that He was going to see me. I could almost audibly hear His Spirit say to me, "Mona, what are you doing?" From that moment, EVERYTHING changed–my school, my friendships, my heart and my outlook. I had a BLESSED HOPE of seeing Jesus one day. I was clean. I was forgiven and ready to live the abundantly – limited regrets. He was mine, I was His–I had salvation. And He is refining me daily.

Write the promise of Philippians 1:6

The next two marching order in 1 Thessalonians 5:11 are (#8) _____ and (#9) _____. I hope and pray I am comforting you and edifying you with these words, "He's not finished working on me." (For all those that know me well, aren't you glad?) Be patient with me. And I'll be with you, because He's still working on you also. It is the hope of our salvation.

He's also coming back for us. Whether we are here or there I'm ready. What will Jesus say when He sees your face? What will you do? What will that face-to-face moment be like? I think about it daily. I am so looking forward to seeing His face and being in His presence. It is truly the hope of my salvation.

Back to our marching orders, Soldier Sis. So far in 1 Thessalonians 5 we have: #1. Don't sleep, #2. Watch, #3. Be sober, #4. Put on the breastplate of faith and love, #5. Put on as a helmet the hope of salvation, # 6. Live with Him, # 7. Comfort each other, and #8. Edify one another.

Since we have salvation and the hope of salvation for the future, we can walk in helpfulness toward others. What marching orders (commands) are listed for us in 1 Thessalonians 12:12-13? #9. _____ #10. _____ and #11. _____

How are you at responding with the mind of Christ when corrections or advice is given to you?

Do you respect, in God's strength, those He has placed over you?

Are you creating a peace among your brothers and sisters in the faith?

Wrap up the list of marching orders by looking at 1 Thessalonians 5:14-22.
(Verse 14) #12._____, #13. _____, #14. _____ and #15. _____.
Which one of those four do you find most challenging to obey? Soldier?
Why?

(Verse 15) #16. _____ But always #17. _____ .
(Verse 16 & 17) #18. _____, and #19 _____.
Both of these are a challenge. How do you think these two can improve simultaneously?

(Verse 18) This is one of the secrets in the Bible. Everyone wonders about it, and now you'll know it. #20. _____.

1 Thessalonians 5:19-22 finishes with a list of five. #21. _____,
#22. _____ , #23. _____ ,
#24. _____ , #25. _____ .

What do you think, Soldier Sis? Do you think you can obey all 25 commands of our Commander-in-Chief? Look back over the list, pray and ask God to show you two specific ones that He desires you to concentrate on today. Write them here.

 Record those two prayer requests, commands, in **Sharpen Your Sword for Week Seven.** Use the references from I Thessalonians 5 as your companion verse(s).

I'd love to close with 1 Thessalonians 5:23-24 as a benediction to today's lesson on marching orders and the Hope of Salvation.

Now may the God of peace himself
sanctify you completely;
and may your whole spirit, soul, and body
be preserved blameless at the coming of our Lord Jesus Christ.
He who calls you is faithful, who also will do it. Amen!

 Review the passage Ephesians 6:10-17 and pray for understanding.

The Perfect Fit

Week Seven   Day Five

My Helmet of Salvation

"And take the helmet of salvation..." Ephesians 6:17

I have been known to clean my house with an actual princess tiara on my head. I vacuum, dust, do dishes and even toilets wearing it around my ponytail. It may not coordinate with my cleaning attire, but I don't care, because it makes me smile, and reminds me of who I am in Christ. I am His. He is mine. Without a doubt, **my helmet is a tiara.**

It sparkles, shines and encourages me to feel like the royal daughter I am. No matter what comes my way, I can imagine having my *tiara of salvation* atop my head. Sometimes, amidst chores in life, I'll get distressed and distracted about my surroundings. I'll forget who I am, what I have, and allow discouragement to set in. Then, the Holy Spirit reminds me of my tiara of salvation. I remember, smile, hold my head high, and walk in God-confidence.

Do I always *feel* like a princess? Absolutely not, but that's only when I forget that my tiara represents my position in Jesus. It is a choice!!! He covers me for He is my helmet of salvation. Am I a *proud* princess? How could I be? My only righteousness comes from God. Am I a *pampered* princess? I am beyond blessed with heavenly blessings.

Having three daughters, I think I have seen all the princess movies, stories and gadgets. I love the storyline of <u>The Little Princess</u>, where the daughter is treated like a princess by her father, but when he is thought to be dead at war, she must resort to poverty. But, in destitution, she remembers who she is, in her father's heart, and that lifts her to dignity. Then there's <u>Princess Diaries</u>, where the awkward young teen discovers she is truly of royal line and becomes the princess she had always been. Who can forget Cinderella, Sleeping Beauty, Snow White, and the rest? Each princess story has a lesson in it for us, ladies—remember to whom you belong. Hold your head high, so your tiara doesn't fall off.

I also love the crowns, tiaras, queens and princess stories in the Bible. There are many. Let's look at two and see what lessons we can apply to our lives from their examples.

The first, and most obvious, crowned woman is Queen Esther. You know the story—there was a need for a new queen and Esther was beautiful and won the Queen Contest. She then learned of a plot to destroy her people, the Jews. She must use her position and power to *do the right thing*. As a daughter of the King, we also have position and power and are obligated to *do the right thing*. Right in the middle of the book of Esther is the pivotal place where Esther must make a decision—literally, life or possible death. Please notice how she used her helmet of salvation, *I mean, her crown*, to think through the situation, accept it, respond and embrace. God has given us a mind, ladies—be sure to use it. Read Esther 4:10-16. What dilemma did Esther face?

> **God has given us a mind, Sisters, be sure to use it.**

How did she accept, respond, and embrace? Or react and endure?

Did her crown make the difference in this situation?

Could she have succeeded if she had not had the crown?

What did she ask Mordecai, all the Jews in Shushan and her maids to do?

Who does this show she is placing her trust in?

You may be at a pivotal place where a wise decision is necessary.

Have you accepted, responded and embraced?

Have you enlisted trusted friends to fast for and with you?

Of the two Biblical queens, Esther was chosen because of her beauty, but what about the other? She was a bit an unlikely queen. Personally, I think I can relate to her much more. May I suggest Rahab from the book of Joshua. Moses had just died, Joshua 1:1, and Joshua is now the earthly leader of the Israelites. God gives Joshua the blessed command and promise of Joshua 1:9. Write it on the lines below and bask in the promise.

(It is one of my favorite verses in the Word and well worth noting and being strengthened by. I find this passage revitalizing, encouraging and powerful. A great sword for striking the enemy. Now, back to the story.)

God commanded Joshua to go over the Jordan River to possess the land, which the Lord had promised them, Joshua 1:11. Joshua sent two men to spy out the land secretly and they came to the house of a harlot named Rahab that lived in Jericho. (Yes, you read that right. The princess in this story was formerly a prostitute. I told you she was *unlikely*.) Rahab's home was visited by the Jericho authorities and she was told to bring them out.

Read what Rahab did in Joshua 2:4-7. Think of three adjectives that describe Rahab's behavior.

Many interpret Rahab differently. She did lie to the authorities, but she protected God's chosen people. Hmmm? Was she brave and courageous, or manipulative and perverted? Good question and I will supply no answer. But, I will give the advice to read the ENTIRE story before you make a judgment call on her. (Which is always good advice, in any situation. Yes?)

Joshua 2:8-9. No internet, television, or radio, yet she had heard quite a bit about the Israelites. How had the Jericho-ites ☺ responded to this information?

According to Joshua 2:9-10, what details had she and others heard about the Israelites?

(The Red Sea miracle was 40 years ago and it was still in the headlines.)
In verses 11-12 we see a part of Rahab's heart. What happened to her heart in verse 11?

What profession of faith does she make in verses 11-12?

How do we know without a doubt that she believed this to be true?

She *knew* the facts about God, *believed* them as truth and then *acted* on them. She thought it through, used her helmet-covered head and decided to put this faith into practice. She knew that in the coming battle, Jericho would lose to Israel. No doubt in that!
What request did she make of the spies in Joshua 2:13?

 Finish reading the story in Joshua 2:14-21. What armor pieces would you say that Rahab was wearing? Circle as many as possible and then write how you believe she appropriated that piece.
Belt of Truth
Breastplate of Righteousness
Shoes of Peace
Shield of Faith

Helmet of Salvation

Sword of the Spirit (The Word of God)

I think she wore the whole armor. Ephesians 6:11 commands us to wear the *whole* armor. We don't get to pick and choose. It's a packaged ensemble. It all coordinates nicely and compliments every part of our lives. Remember, it's a perfect fit.

 Write beside each what blessing she received for wearing the armor.

Matthew 1:5   Hebrews 11:31   James 2:25

She became a grandmother of Jesus and King David (this is where the royalty fits in), she was noted for her faith (this is where the salvation fits in) and she was justified by her works.

Two very different women wore their helmets of salvation in the battles of life. Both women were chosen by God for their particular mission. He placed the tiaras on their heads and they appropriated them to honor their God. You may find the choices required of a Godly, tiara-wearing woman difficult. So what about you? Are you sporting a *tiara of salvation*?

So, here I am in my defensive armor. It looks a little different than a Roman soldier, but it is who I am in Christ—a woman with a golden belt of truth and a pure white breastplate of righteousness that covers me completely. My dancing shoes of peace allow me to literally float in the Spirit, light on my feet since I am at peace with my God. My dented shield of faith protects me completely when I use it in God's strength. And now with my tiara of salvation atop my head, not only is it beautiful, but also practical as it keeps my mind stayed on Him. As I put on each piece – piece, by piece, by piece, and find myself in His presence, I want to cast my crowns at His feet and say,

"Holy, Holy, Holy, Lord, God Almighty,

Who was and is and is to come.

You are worthy, O Lord, to receive glory and honor and power.

For you created all things,

And by Your will they exist and were created."

Would you join me? I can see your tiara sparkling from here.

 Be sure to add a praise in **Sharpen Your Sword for Week Seven.** Hallelujah!

 Wow! You have memorized Ephesians 6:10-17. Read it aloud, then recite it imagining every personalized piece on you. *You look beautiful.*

Sharpen Your Sword

Week Seven

Concern	Truth to Believe	Date	Answer
A worry	Proverbs 3:5-6 "He will direct my paths."		

The Perfect Fit

Week Seven Wrap-Up

Principal Questions for Week Seven

1. Why are we separated from God? (Isaiah 59:1-3. 2)

2. Genesis 3:1-5; what did Satan question and why?

3. According to 2 Corinthians 10:4, what weapons do we use to fight spiritual warfare?

4. Which commands of God are found in 1 Thessalonians 5:19-22?

5. Name the blessings Rahab received for putting on God's armor

Matthew 1:5

Hebrews 11:31

James 2:25

Practical Questions for Week Seven

1. When God feels far away, who has moved?

2. What do you think went through Eve's mind before she ate the forbidden fruit?

3. What actions aid in your obedience to Christ?

4. Which two of the 25 commands of God should you make a priority right now?

5. When have you needed to step out in deep faith as Rahab did?

Session Eight – The Sword of the Spirit

Ephesians 6:17b "and take the sword of the Spirit, which is the Word of God."

*Heb 4:12   *Mark 16:15   *Psalm 119:105   *Romans 10:17   *Rev 1:3   *Acts 17:11

The Roman soldier's sword was crafted from iron. It is the only offensive weapon mentioned. It protected the soldier from the enemy, defeated the enemy's plan and rescued lives. It was usually between 6-18 inches and used in hand-to-hand combat. Swords were stored in an armory, *mach-aira*. (Mt 26:47, 51; Acts 12:2; Heb 11:37)

1.   The Sword is powerful and _____.

The _____ has no ability to understand the things of God. (I Cor 2:14)

2.   Christ is the _____ and example to us on how to fight.

A victory – baptism (Matthew 3:13-17)

A battle – fully dressed in armor (Matthew 4:1-11) Devil left.

        A great sword fight!

A ministry – God is glorified (Matthew 4:12 and on)

"He was clothed with a robe dipped in blood, and His name is called ___ _____ ___ _____."

Revelation 19:1-16   (Logos)

Why do we fight with the Sword of the Spirit?

We fight **not** to win at Bible Trivia, to win a great discussion or to prove a point, but to _____ ____ _____ in our lives, in our relationships and in the lives of those we love. We fight to live victoriously.

Share some of your most-used swords that you have used in battle. Pray them over a situation.

The Perfect Fit

Week Eight   Day One

The Sword of the Spirit

*"...And take the helmet of salvation, and the **sword of the Spirit**, which is the Word of God."*
Ephesians 6:17

As we begin Week Eight, we find ourselves fully suited in the armor of God. As for me, I have the belt of truth (gold sash), breastplate of righteousness (white and sparkling flowing gown), shoes of peace (white ballet slippers), shield of faith (large and well-worn glistening shield) and helmet of salvation (diamond studded tiara). Yours may look different, but power is of God, through Jesus. Each fit is custom for us and practical to protect us from the fiery darts of the wicked. We can stand in this armor. Through experience, we've learned how. Actually, after we become accustomed to them, we can dance and worship fully dressed. I can't help but believe that the Lord is pleased with our progress and now He hands us one last armor piece... the sword of the Spirit.

I can see it all in my imagination and am humbled as the sword is placed in my hands. With the gift of the Sword, comes the understanding that I will learn how to use it against the enemy. This week we will look at what this Sword represents and how we can practically appropriate this magnificent armor piece to glorify our God and defeat the enemies in our lives.

As Paul was describing the Roman armor piece by piece, he named and assigned a spiritual quality or characteristic to each. Yet, the sword is the only one that he defines for us. The Sword of the Spirit IS the Word of God. There is no doubt to how the sword is to be interpreted. Let's begin by looking at the Roman sword.

The Greek word for sword, *macharia,* is written in the following verses. Look up each and write a description of the use of the swords mentioned.

Matthew 26:47, 51   Acts 12:2   Hebrews 11:37

In the above verses the sword was used to destroy, cut and bring harm. Likewise, we are to use it as a weapon. J. Gordon Henry, in his book, <u>Spiritual Warfare</u>, says, "A material sword pierces the body; the spiritual sword pierces the heart. The material sword becomes dull by use; the spiritual sword becomes sharper as it is used. The physical sword wounds to hurt; the spiritual sword pierces to heal. The physical sword demands the hand of the one who uses it; the Word of God does not need anything, but it carries its own power.

The term *machaira* refers to the normal sword carried by Roman soldiers of the day. Different commentators describe it as anything from a six-inch dagger to a two-foot sword. It was put into a sheath or a scabbard on the side of the soldier and was used in hand-to-hand combat. It was a precise weapon that needed to be used in a precise way to be effective in hand-to-hand combat.[1] Understanding this weapon, a Christian woman can gain insight into the nature of the spiritual sword she must wield. This double-edged Roman sword was a fierce and dangerous weapon.[1] The short sword also had a double-edged blade and was a terrible stabbing weapon. It was short enough to wield easily in the crush of battle and devastatingly effective. It was designed to penetrate and disembowel the enemy. It was well known that if a Roman soldier ever unsheathed his sword—he would use it.[2]

> **The material sword becomes dull by use, the spiritual sword becomes sharper as it is used.**

Dangerous? Terrible? Powerful? Yes.
There is nothing pretty, dainty, or delicate.

We're talking the most deadly weapon imaginable. And, Sisters, it is at our disposal.

Have I frightened you? That is not my intent, but I do hope I bring the reality of the warfare we fight to the forefront of your thinking.

 Our sword of the Spirit is crafted, tempered and honed by none other than the Holy Spirit Himself. Note what is recorded about the *Word of God*, in the Word of God.

Proverbs 30:5   Luke 4:4   1 John 2:14

We have a spiritual sword to use in spiritual combat, because the Holy Spirit gave it to us. It is the Word spoken by the Spirit as He brings *alive* words from the printed page. Learning how to use it effectively is totally dependent upon how diligently we get involved in studying the Bible. Whether we become an excellent swordsman or maintain mediocrity is entirely our choice. It is dependent upon whether we exercise the discipline required.

There are two different terms in Greek for *word;* one is *logos* and the other, *rhema.* The word *logos* usually means *as a whole* and common passages where *logos* is used is in John 1:1-8 and Revelation 19:13. In these verses, the Word is capitalized because this is the *logos* of God in His Son, Jesus Christ. Most of the time the word *rhema* refers to a specific statement or utterance.

The sword of the Spirit is not the *logos,* but the *rhema,* an individual text or saying of the Word. So we would read the verse accurately like the following:

> *"...take the sword of the Spirit which is the **rhema** of God."* Ephesians 6:17

This may be an oversimplification, but, I like to think of going to the armory (the Word or *logos*), and getting a saying of God or sayings of God (the word or *rhema*). Swords are stored at various places in the armory and we need to know the sayings to be able to use them appropriately. The *rhema* of God is the saying or sayings of God applied to specific situations. When I recall a verse to use as a weapon against the enemy, I've taken one sword from the whole armory. The next time I need a different verse, I take another sword.

Let's see how it works by carefully examination Hebrews 4:12:

> *"For the word of God is living and powerful, and sharper than any two-edged sword, piercing even to the division of soul and spirit, and of joints and marrow, and is a discerner of the thoughts and intents of the heart."*

When we consider the Word as a *rhema,* or sword from the armory, the Holy Spirit gives it life—it is living and powerful. The words God speaks are <u>spirit and life</u>.

Read and record John 6:63.

> ## The words God speaks are spirit and life.

Like an expert surgeon can cut flesh and organs, the words of God can divide our soul and spirit. Which would you think is easier to do? Divide our flesh and bone or divide our soul and spirit? 2 Timothy 3:14-16 is key to knowledge of the Sword's capacity.

When should we begin learning?

Verse 16 says, *"All scripture is given by inspiration of God."* Always know that *all means all* and that *inspiration* is interpreted as *God-breathed*. Remember, God having a discussion about you in the heavenlies from Week Two? He breathed your name. But the entire Bible, from Genesis to Revelation is God-breathed. He spoke the words to His children and they put it down on paper. Every word is inspired and anointed by the holiness of God.

Let's look at all God's Word—continuing in verse 16.
God's Word is -

"profitable for doctrine"—for teaching

"for reproof"—for conviction

"for correction"—setting things right in your life

"for instruction in righteousness"—thinking and acting in God's will

It is given so that "the man of God", or woman of God, *"may be complete, thoroughly equipped for every good work."*

 Can you think of a couple things in your life that you would like to be complete and thoroughly equipped for? (I could make a list!) We have all we need to offensively fight in battle.

 Sharpen Your Sword for Week Eight by writing a prayer request with a sword from the armory for battle.

 Read Ephesians 6:10-17. Note the flow from verse to verse.

The Perfect Fit

Week Eight   Day Two

The Master Swordsman

"...And take the helmet of salvation and the sword of the Spirit, which is the Word of God."
Ephesians 6:17

"Necessity is the mother of invention." My mom used that quote often as she created a new way to solve a problem. If we didn't have the money to buy book covers, she would use paper bags. If we didn't have any glue or paste, she would mix flour and water. Run out of toothpaste? Try Mom's homemade brand made out of baking soda. I find myself now trying to solve problems in my home the same way. Necessity is truly the mother of invention. The one who invents or designs a product or instrument knows best how to use it.

As humans, we have a problem and need a way to defeat the spiritual wickedness in high places, so that we can walk victoriously. So God provided His Son, Jesus, as the Redeemer for our sin. Jesus' birth, death and resurrection are enough. Yet, God knew we would need a daily weapon to defeat the enemy in our day-to-day struggles. So, we have His Word, the Sword of the Spirit. For us to understand the use of the Sword of the Spirit, we as need only look at the Lord Jesus. He spoke and wrote the Word, created a "way of escape,"–1 Corinthians 10:13, and left a detailed record of how to accomplish this in Matthew four.

Matthew three tells the story of when John the Baptist baptized Jesus.
Let's glory in the moment in Matthew 3:13-17.
What did John try to prevent Jesus from doing in verses 13-14?

Why do you think he did?

What did Jesus respond in verse 15?

> **Jesus' birth, death and resurrection are enough.**

When Jesus came up from the water, what happened according to verses 16-17?

Baptisms are incredible times of commitment, decision and change. Jesus was committed to obeying the father. He knew it was His time to put down His carpentry tools and pick up His Father's call on His life—to walk toward the cross. Jesus voiced His choice and then acted upon it. The Father was pleased with His commitment. Perhaps you are at a place of growth and change in your spiritual journey. If you have diligently sought God's Word and His will over the past several weeks, He has been speaking to you, too.

Jesus heard from His Father, God Himself, *"This is My beloved Son, in whom I am well pleased."* He knew He was where His Father had led Him. He was on the right path and it was His passion to do His Father's will. He had been physically separated from His father for 30 years and now He hears His voice. Can you imagine the intimacy the two shared? It must have been an incredible moment for our Lord Jesus and the Father.

As if we were watching a movie, the music turns to a minor key, the light darkens and we sense something horrible is on the way. But this is neither fiction nor Hollywood; it is the true story of the enemy of our soul tempting our Savior.

 According to Matthew 4:1-2, who led Jesus into the wilderness? _____ Do you find that conflicting? Why? Why not?

 The Spirit was responsible for both the testing and the 40-day fast. A *tempting* is a testing to demonstrate our faithfulness and develop our character. It does not always result in a negative outcome, especially when you're wearing the full armor of God. For when we are wearing our full armor, we are prepared in the Spirit to be victorious. There can only be conquest and victory when there is combat and struggle. Of course, Jesus was wearing His full armor, but please don't minimize this temptation thinking it was easy because He was God. He was all God, but all man also.

What do the verses Hebrews 2:18 and 4:15 have to say about Jesus being tempted?

This was truly a trial. He was physically weak and yet miraculously victorious, by using the Sword of the Spirit. Three holy Sword fights evolved.

Sword fight One

Read Matthew 4:3-4.

What was the first temptation? Oh, how we as women can relate to this one. Ever been tempted by food?

Ever know you shouldn't eat something, for whatever reason, and yet you find yourself tempted? Ever sneak food? Ever lie about what you ate? To yourself or others?

You know what I'm talking about. Food is a temptation to us. But can you imagine after forty days of not eating? I can't. The Master Swordsman, Jesus, defeats the enemy with a word. What does Jesus answer in Matthew 4:4?

"It is written." Try vocalizing that phrase before a promise the next time you are struggling. Jesus would not turn the stones to bread because God had not lead Him to. He would not obey Satan no matter how hungry He was.

Sister, _God's Word is practical for our daily trials and temptations._

Sword fight Two

Read Matthew 4:5-7.
What was the second temptation?

Power and pride. Can we relate to these as women?

Ever been tempted by pride? Ever think more highly of yourself than you ought?

Ever exaggerate a story, just a tad, to make yourself seem stronger, smarter or wiser?

Sadly, I confess, I have been guilty of that very thing. I was tempted and yielded to it.

I am weak, but I can find strength when reading a *sword* from 2 Corinthians 12:9-10. What is it?

Is there a promise in there for you to use against the enemy?

Learn to sharpen your sword so you are ready to battle the enemy. Jesus is our example.

What does Jesus answer in Matthew 4:7?

How does pride in ourselves defeat us in our Christian walk?

How does Satan gain the victory in our lives?

"It is written." Vocalize that the next time you are tempted to brag on yourself and follow it with Luke 14:11. What is the sword you can use in the armory of Luke 14:11?

God's Word is practical for our everyday trials and temptations.

Sword fight Three

Read Matthew 4:8-10.
What was the third temptation?

Worshipping the world in place of God. Can we relate to this one? *Worship* means to glorify, magnify and lift up; it is intended for God alone. Have you ever been tempted to worship the creation instead of the Creator? Our children and/or husband, instead of the One that gave them to us? To worship vacation, wealth or personal talent, instead of the Giver of all gifts?

What does Satan gain when he shoots us with these fiery darts and the darts penetrate our hearts?

What armor piece could help us in this battle?

The Master Swordsman again goes to the Old Testament armory and gathers a sword.
What was Jesus' response in Matthew 4:10?

"It is written." Vocalize that, right out loud, the next time you are tempted to worship, prioritize, or exalt your job, children, or talent. Follow it with Deuteronomy 6:13 that reads:

Here is the power to get our worship back where it belongs. When we find ourselves focusing our attention and magnification more on the things around us than the God of all, we need to get our focus back onto the Lord. Satan would love nothing more than to get us thinking about the cares, worries, concerns and even the good things in this life. They can be blessings, but we must remember from where good things come.
What does James 1:17 remind us about this fact?

<u>God's Word is practical for our everyday trials and temptations.</u>

When living triumphantly in God's presence, we can expect combat, trials, fiery darts, tribulation and discouragement. It's all part of the spiritual battle we fight. In Matthew 4:1-11, Jesus gives us His example, and I rejoice with verse eleven.

Write what two major things happened in this one little verse?

"The devil left Him." We know the devil returned, but for now, he left Him. The enemy was defeated with three strikes of the sword. All praise to God alone!!

What promise can we practice in James 4:7?

 Soldier Sis, we have been given the same sword to use in battle against him. It carries the same power. When is the last time you picked up the sword to fight the enemy?

Be very honest in answering that question.

Are you in the practice of quoting scripture to thwart the enemy when moments of temptations and trials come your way?

Do you believe it would bring you victory if you did? _____
If it's been a while since you found yourself in a swordfight with the enemy, why not today write down one promise from the Word of God and be ready to wield it.

I love the picture of the full armor of God. My left hand holds my shield of faith and my right, the sword of the Spirit. That means I have no hands free to give to the enemy to be led astray. When I do put down my sword to rest, it should only be to hold on to the hand of God. I picture it in my mind that way. When that happens, the devil leaves, and angels come to minister to me. It is an amazing moment.

Isn't that what happened to our Lord Jesus? *"The devil left Him and angels came to minister to Him."* Jesus won the swordfight because He used the power of the Word of God that was provided for Him. He overcame Satan by using the individual Scriptures that God provided in the armory. Christ defeated Satan by using the sword of the Spirit. He resisted the devil and the devil left Him. (Matthew 4:11, James 4:7)

**Through His death, burial, resurrection and ascension, Christ
defeated Satan completely, and Jesus' victory is ours through faith.**

Read that sentence one hundred times until you understand the meaning.

It was complete, not just for one temptation.

> **I have no hands free to give to the enemy.**

Read the following verses and write the victory that is ours.

Colossians 2:13-15

Ephesians 1:19-23

We can never defeat God's enemies or win God's battle without God's Book.

 Record any prayer requests today in the **Sharpen Your Sword for Week Eight.**

 Read Ephesians 6:10-17. Now try to say it all from memory. You can do it!

The Perfect Fit

Week Eight   Day Three

Planting the Seed

*"...And take the helmet of salvation, and the **sword of the Spirit**, which is the Word of God."*
Ephesians 6:17

This summer I planted a garden. It was four rows of tomatoes, peppers, cucumbers, radishes, eggplant, a variety of squash and a random okra plant. I had absolutely no idea what I was doing, but I was up for the challenge. I prepared the ground by hand, pulling out weeds and rocks. I put in nine tomato plants and four eggplant plants that had been given to me. I was so proud. I still had plenty of prepared soil so I went to the local gardening store and bought a variety of seeds for summer vegetables. I was clueless about what varieties to buy, so I just randomly chose what seemed interesting. I attempted to plant them, as instructed, then sat back in my recliner to admire my work. There was no fruit for my labor yet, just plants and seeds in the ground. I was thrilled!

I spent many hours in my garden. Some hours were spent watering. Many hours I just enjoyed the quiet garden surroundings, away from the phone and housework, in prayer, meditation and reading. Then, there were many, MANY hours spent weeding. I made tons of gardening mistakes and would be humbled by any real gardener walking within a thousand feet of my garden, but honestly, I can say I enjoyed the entire process. I've reaped some odd shaped vegetables and am still trying to figure out what to do with the okra. What I reaped the most, though, were lessons about reaping and sowing.

Interestingly, the more rain that fell, the more weeding was necessary. I could weed the entire garden today, water tomorrow, and find new weeds the next. I was amazed at the tenacity of the weeds. Some even had flowers and were quite lovely, but they were weeds, nonetheless, and they had to go. Spiritual applications grew daily and especially ones from Jesus' parable of the Sower and the Seed.

As we continue to study the sword of the Spirit, which is the Word of God, I think it would be to our benefit to study the parable of the Sower and the Seed.

Let's look at Matthew 13:1-4. Describe the scene?

Use your imagination and picture the activity of the setting. Can you feel the motion of the boat on the water? Can you hear the water lapping along the shore? Are the people gathered seated in groups, standing or do they have their lawn chairs reclined? What do their faces look like? Imagine it.

Know that it had been a long day for Jesus. He was about halfway through His teaching years and was gathering quite a following. He had been busy about His Father's business all day long. Glance at Matthew eleven and twelve.

Matthew 13:4 introduces us to a parable. Rabbis of the day used parables and stories to teach truth. It was a teaching method using common scenes from everyday life to teach a new lesson about the kingdom. The passage doesn't mention it, but I believe a garden was visible from the teaching spot in the boat. Perhaps even a farmer was planting. Can you picture it?

Jesus begins by telling the story of the sower in Matthew 13:3-9. Read the parable He told and imagine yourself there on the shore. Write a few notes about each of the different kinds of soil and what happened to the seed that fell there.

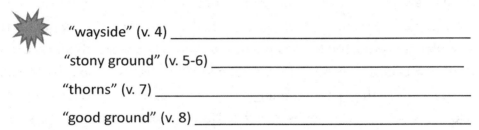

"wayside" (v. 4) _____

"stony ground" (v. 5-6) _____

"thorns" (v. 7) _____

"good ground" (v. 8) _____

I love the honesty of Matthew 13:10. Read it. What do the disciples ask?

While teaching, I enjoy immensely the questions of my students. When they are asking questions, they are with me and actively learning. It's an exciting time. It's learning at its best. Jesus must have been thrilled with their question. The Master Teacher continues with the answer in Matthew thirteen. Notice how the beginning of this chapter is divided. In Matthew 13:1-9 Jesus tells all those listening on the shore the parable of the sower. In the next few verses, Matthew 13:10-17, He gives the purpose for the use of parables. In Matthew 13:18-23 Jesus explains the meaning of the parable of the sower.

Read Matthew 13:10-17 and see why Jesus spoke in the parables. It seemed that Jesus' enemies rejected His teachings. The multitudes were interested, but only in the miracles, not the personal spiritual applications. Jesus used this teaching method as a design to reveal spiritual truths in a way that those who were eager to understand could. Not only could they understand the spiritual truth being discussed, but look at verses 12-13.

In what way would those who desire spiritual things understand?

I find this thrilling. Not only could they understand, they would understand more and more. Do you realize that includes us? Oh, my goodness, I can feel the Holy Spirit rising up inside me. *In abundance* is how verse twelve puts it in the NKJV. Basically, the more we are in the Word, the more we understand spiritual things. The more we pray for understanding, the more the Lord will provide it. The more we use the sword of the Spirit, the better we get at wielding it. On the contrary, those that do not hunger and thirst after righteousness, those that do not seek spiritual insight, will not understand them.

According to Matthew 13:16, what will we be when we see, hear and understand these spiritual truths?

Let's not forget that Jesus is the one speaking here. He is truth and can only speak truth. Here we are able to read His Word and have the Holy Spirit live within us. We are so blessed!

We've read the parable. We know why Jesus taught using parables. Now, let's look at His explanation of this particular one in Matthew 13:18-23. Read on, Sister.

The *seed* is the perfect, powerful, infallible Word of God — our Sword of the Spirit. Jesus explained that when the Word was shared on the <u>wayside</u> it did not take root because the *ground*, the heart of the unbeliever, was indifferent to the Word. When the Word was shared on the <u>stony ground</u>, there was no root in her heart so at the first wind of trouble she forgets the Word and goes back to living in the flesh. The cares of the world steal the Sword of the Spirit from the woman with a heart like the <u>thorny ground</u>. But, the woman on the <u>good ground</u>, a heart ready to receive the Word, produces fruit.

The condition of anyone's soil or heart determines the potential they have for growth. The unbeliever and the believer can relate to the same principle. There are times when I hear the Word of God, yet am not prepared to grow from it. Satan has no control over whether I hear it or not, that is entirely my choice. I can choose to focus on the cares of this world and not embrace the Word of God. Oh, may I have a heart ready to receive the Word of God.

Even though I am far from an excellent gardener, the good seed that I planted yielded fruit. (Perhaps it was odd-shaped, but it was fruit none-the-less.) When we surrender and allow the Perfect Gardener to work our soil with His seed, the Word of God, a harvest will grow! Be encouraged! We do reap what we sow.

 Be sure to **Sharpen Your Sword for Week Eight**.

 Find a fellow Soldier to recite Ephesians 6:10-17 to today.

The Perfect Fit

Week Eight   Day Four

The Life-Changing Instruction Guide

"...And take the helmet of salvation, and the sword of the Spirit which is the Word of God."
Ephesians 6:17

This powerful Sword of the Spirit that you hold in your hands is life changing. Believe that and build your life upon it. It is the only offensive weapon we have to fight the enemy when he attempts to make us stumble. We must use the precious Sword of the Spirit, the infallible Word of God, as if our life depends upon it. Our life *does*.

We have spent much time in the Word of God. We know it is living, powerful and inspired by God. It is God-breathed and for our benefit by dividing our thoughts and the intents of our hearts. Listening to and obeying the Word wins the battles in our lives. The more we are in the Word of God, under the guidance of the Holy Spirit, the more we understand spiritual things. The more we understand spiritual things, the more we KNOW that God is in control and working for our best.

Psalm 119.

This lengthy Psalm of 176 verses celebrates the Word of God. It is an acrostic poem; for each of the twenty-two consonants in the Hebrew alphabet, there are eight verses beginning with that letter. Within the Psalm, eight words for God's Law occur again and again: *law; testimonies; promise; precepts; statutes; commandments; judgments* and *word*. The Psalm uses the full meaning of all these words as it elaborates on the application of the Law of God to both daily life and Israel's destiny. The psalmist cannot stop praising God for His mercy and goodness in providing His people with instructions for living.[1]

We cannot look at every verse, idea or even theme in this the longest chapter in the Bible, but let's read through Psalm 119 highlighting some themes that relate to us as soldiers learning to use the sword of the Spirit. Let's treat this Psalm as an instruction guide on the how's and why's of wielding the Sword of the Spirit.

Read Psalm 119:1-8. Of the eight words for the sword of the Spirit or the Word of God: law, testimonies, promise, precepts, statutes, commandments, judgments and the word; how many are mentioned in verses 1-8?

The words are synonyms for God's Revelation to man. The *law* is God's instruction from Moses to the prophets, usually determined as the first 5 books of the Old Testament. *Statutes* are things inscribed, noting the word's permanence. The *testimonies* are ordinances or God's standard of conduct according to the Ten Commandments. The pattern of life required by God's law is the *way*. *Precepts* and *commandments* are required orders from an authority. A binding law is a *judgment*. The word, *word,* as used in Ephesians 6:17 is a general term that encompasses all of the terms. Although each individual word carries a significant meaning; in general we understand together they represent the sword of the Spirit. Understanding these terms we can use this magnificent sword more appropriately.

Read Psalm 119:1-8 again. Why are the hearers of the word blessed?
Note the many actions or verbs happening. Record the phrases below verse by verse.

Verse 1 ____walk in the law_____   Verse 2 ____keep His testimonies____

Verse 3 _____   Verse 4 _____

Verse 5 _____   Verse 6 _____

Verse 7 _____and _____

Verse 8 _____

 According to the beginning of this Psalm, as soldiers in the Lord's army, how do we appropriate this Sword? Is it by hearing and reading only?

Some expositors interpret Psalm 119:11 by specifically looking at "in my heart." Yes, we use our mind to memorize but "my heart" requires love and a willingness to obey. We must have a heart's desire to please Him. The principles of His Word must be hidden in our hearts. When God's Word is part of us, we are in love with the Author, we do not sin against Him and we know to defeat the enemy using the Sword of the Spirit.

We will walk in the law, keep His testimonies, seek Him with our whole heart, and hide the Word in our hearts. What does Psalm 119:13 tell us to do with the Sword of the Spirit?

How about verse 14?
What are we supposed to do with God's precepts in verse 15?

Psalm 119:16 reminds us to delight ourselves in the Word and to "not forget" it. Not forgetting carries the idea of putting God's Word to memory.

 We will speak or <u>declare</u> His Word, <u>rejoice</u> in God's way, and <u>meditate</u> on His precepts. Of those three, which do you find easiest to do?
Which is most difficult?

Why do you believe that is so?

Do you consider speaking, rejoicing and meditating on God's Word commands?

How do we benefit from obeying God's Word?

How does following these instructions better equip us as soldiers in the Lord's army?

> **Don't wait for the enemy to attack or the battle to begin ... Strike first!**

When it is our heart's desire to have the Word of God fill our every part, what does Psalm 119:32 say God will do for us?
God keeps giving and giving.

Read Psalm 119:37.
Can you think of a few *worthless things* that may take your time instead of the Word?

> **Physical life to live for Him.
> Eternal life to live with Him.
> Abundant life to live victoriously in the power of God – everyday.**

When struggles come our way, what does Psalm 119:50 say God's Word will be for us?

Psalm 119:105 is probably the most familiar of all the verses in this chapter. What does it say to you as you consider your role as a soldier in the Lord's army?

Do you love the Word of God as we are encouraged to in Psalm 119:127?

Can you think of things you may love more? Any *gold* in your life that is better than the Word?

As we look at this life-changing instruction book, from Psalm 119, we gain a list of things we are to do. Each of these is a way to learn accurately how to wield this Sword of the Spirit to its fullest potential for our lives. Let's conclude with Psalm 119:50 and Psalm 119:93.

What do both of these verses say God's Word gives us?

Physical life to live for Him.

Eternal life to live with Him.

Abundant life is to live victoriously in the power of God—everyday. Don't wait for the enemy to strike, use this offensive weapon and strike first!

Write down your prayer requests in **Sharpen Your Swords for Week Eight**. Try to include a verse from Psalm 119.

Continue to memorize the passage Ephesians 6:10-17. Write verse seventeen below.

The Perfect Fit

Week Eight   Day Five

My Sword of the Spirit

*"...And take the helmet of salvation and the **sword of the Spirit**, which is the Word of God."*
Ephesians 6:17

*S*everal years ago I had a friend tell me about her thrill of sharing a flight with the Christian music artist, Sandi Patty. I appreciated my friend's enthusiasm and shared in her excitement, but hours later I remember thinking, "So what? I can spend every morning conversing with the Creator of the Universe." I smiled, then thought, "I can, but do I?"

Do I? I have opportunity to daily have a private briefing with God. As I read His Word and wait on the Holy Spirit for understanding, I can hear directly from the heart of God. I can, but do I? He is actively discerning my thoughts and dividing my soul and spirit, as stated in Hebrews 4:12. I can receive instruction in righteous living by the very Giver of Life as described in 2 Timothy 3:16. I can, but do I? Reading the Word of God and obeying His commands is the only way I can become a Godly woman ready to fight the enemy in the battles of life. I can, and I must. I must choose, minute by minute, to be victorious, receive, and activate this gift provided.

God has provided for you and me, a Sword, His Word, to use in every spiritual battle that comes our way. I'd like to share with you a simple device to aid us in appropriating the Sword. I did not originate this clever visual, but find it excellent for teaching this topic of how to handle the sword of the Spirit.

Take your sword, your Bible, in one hand. Grip it with all four fingers, your thumb and even the palm of your hand. Now, place it down and try to pick it up with your thumb only. Your thumb represents the first way to handle the Sword of the Spirit— ***Hearing God's Word***. Every Sunday, as you fellowship with other believers, you hear the Word. You become acquainted with the content.

I can, but do I?

What does Romans 10:17 say about hearing the Word of God?

It is hearing the Word and being sensitive to the leading of the Holy Spirit that leads us to repentance and salvation. We must first hear the Word, but can we grow if we hear it only? Why or why not?

Now, let's add your pointer finger to the visual. Try picking up your Bible with your thumb and pointer. It can be done, but you do not have full control of the sword in your hand. The pointer finger represents your second step in learning how to handle the sword of the Spirit—***Reading God's Word***. This is what I try to do every morning during my Quiet Time with the Lord. I read the Word and pray for understanding.

What does Revelation 1:3 say we will be if we read the Word?

Again, I ask you to place your Bible down and attempt to pick it up using your thumb, pointer finger and middle finger. The middle finger represents your third step in learning how to handle the sword of the Spirit—***Studying God's Word***. Reading the Word daily takes discipline, but studying the Word takes real concerted effort. This is where we really begin to make the Word our own. This is not just hearing the Word and reading it for yourself, but comparing scriptures to scriptures and researching topics and attending Bible studies and asking questions. This is interacting with the Word. It is where we really begin to sharpen our sword.

What example are we given in Acts 17:11?

This is a disciplined step toward spiritual maturity.

Try to pick up your Bible again, now using your thumb, pointer, middle finger and ring finger. The ring finger is the fourth step in learning how to handle the sword of the Spirit—***Memorizing God's Word***. Now we are talking discipline. When the enemy is permitted to place trying times in our path, we can defeat him by quoting a memorized promise from God's Word.

Let me give you an example.

Read Proverbs 7:2-3. (I especially like the Living Bible translation of this one.) What is God telling you to do with His precious Word?

The other day I was feeling quite alone. I found myself beginning to worry about a situation with one of our daughters. I wanted to share it with someone, but felt I could not and still hold complete confidentiality. I was concerned about how it was all going to play out. Then, as I was driving, my heart and mind was reminded of Jeremiah 33:3. *"Call to me and I will answer you and show you great and mighty things which you do not know."* Because I had placed that verse in my memory, it was there to recall and comfort me in my time of need. I realized that I could share it all with God and He had a reason and purpose for each part of the situation. The enemy attempted to test my faith, but I used the sword of the Spirit, named "Jeremiah 33:3" to thwart his plans. I was immediately filled with the comfort of the Holy Spirit. Battle won! Victory was mine!

Meditating on God's Word is the fifth step in learning how to handle the sword of the Spirit. Try picking up your Bible using your thumb and all four fingers, including the pinky. Do not use your palm at all. You have pretty good control, but still lacking a bit. It would be like trying to cut a large piece of meat holding the knife with your fingertips only; limited control is possible. Meditating on God's Word is when we read, hear, study and then really think on it.

According to Psalm 1:1-3, what happens when we meditate on the law of God?

Our final and sixth step in learning how to properly use the sword of the Spirit is ***Applying God's Word***. This is using our entire hand, including our palm to grab the sword and appropriate it against the enemy. It's really *knowing* the Word and expertly using the sword on a daily basis in your everyday life. It's living out the Word of God. Applying God's Word is done with a willing heart and a deep love for obedience.

   What does Matthew 5:19 say we will be called when we apply God's commands?

What?! Me? Called that? The Word says it, so I believe it, by faith.

   How can properly handling this dangerous, yet glorious weapon, change the way you fight the battles of life?

The more I hear, read, study, memorize, meditate and practice God's Word, the more I realize I know so little. God's Word and character is so much broader than my little mind can comprehend. That's why I trust Him. He is greater than my need, knows my beginning from my end, and separates my sin from me as far as the east is from the west. My Commander-in-Chief speaks to me through His Word and directs me on how to live... abundantly. Once I know how to handle my Sword of the Spirit, I am the one that receives all the benefits and victorious living.

Piece by piece by piece we receive each part of this magnificent armor of God. Truth. Righteousness. Peace. Faith. Salvation. And, now, His Word. This gift is mine and yours. <u>I can</u> have intimacy with the Creator of the Universe, through His Word. <u>I can.</u> <u>You can.</u> This final piece of armor, this powerful sword of the Spirit, is ours for the taking and using effectively. Like you, I must woman-up daily, choose life, and fight, with the only real power available to me – the sword of the Spirit. <u>In the power of God, we can.</u>

> **I must woman-up daily, choose life, and fight with the Sword.**

 Write your prayer request(s) for today on the **Sharpen Your Sword for Week Eight**. Be sure to include a sword to use in battle.

 State aloud Ephesians 6:10-17. Reflect on the power, promise and praise offered to you, Soldier Sis!

The Perfect Fit

Sharpen Your Sword

Week Eight

Concern	Truth to Believe	Date	Answer
A worry	Proverbs 3:5-6 "He will direct my paths."		

The Perfect Fit

Week Eight Wrap-Up

Principal Questions for Week Eight

1. What is recorded about the *Word of God*, in the Word of God?

Proverbs 30:5

Luke 4:4

1 John 2:14

2. What do Hebrews 2:18 and 4:15 have to say about Jesus wilderness temptation

3. Explain the four soils and reactions of the seed in Matthew 13:3-9.

4. What does Psalm 119:1-8 say about your use of the Word of God (Sword)?

5. What does Matthew 5:19 say we will be called when we apply God's commands to our lives?

Practical Questions for Week Eight

1. Can you think of a couple things in your life you need to be complete and thoroughly equipped for?

2. Do you find a conflict in God allowing temptation into Spiritual testing?

3. What differences do you think an observer and a believer would see in the parable of the sower?

4. Do you consider speaking, rejoicing and meditating on God's Word a command?

5. How careful are you in the handling of God's Word?

The Perfect Fit

Session Nine – The Battle of Prayer

" … Praying always with all prayers and supplication in the Spirit, being watchful to this end with all perseverance and supplication for all the saints." Ephesians 6:18-20

Hebrews 4: 16 We are invited to the _____ _____.
Jeremiah 29:11-13 The _____ wants to hear us.
John 14:13-14 It _____!

"Praying always" … **Constantly in prayer**

> The enemy watches for the _____ of believers, and then attacks.
> Prayer should be as natural as _____.

"…with all prayer and supplication" … **all** Phil 4:6-7 Matt 18:20 w/ others, private,

> Corporate, audible, silent, meetings, songs, worship, praise, tears, surrender

> **Prayer will release a power from Heaven on our behalf that far surpasses the power of those who are against us.**

ACTS – A _____
C _____
T _____
S _____

"in the Spirit" … *the POWER*
Perfect Harmony!

The moment we begin to pray, both the _____ and _____ pray.

"being watchful to this end" … Col 4:2 Neh 4:9
We must be _____.
Where do the Drowsies, Daydreams, Distractions come from?

"with all perseverance" … Romans 12:12
Hold on. Hold out. Not faint. Not quit. Not yield to discouragement, by _____.
We do not want to become _____ of _____..

The Perfect Fit

Week Nine   Day One

The Battlefield

"...Praying always with all prayer and supplication in the Spirit, being watchful to this end with all perseverance and supplication for all the saints..." Ephesians 6:18

I'll never forget my first day of school—as the teacher. I had just finished four years of intense study. I knew the details of child and adolescent psychology, researched hours on methods of reading, had a solid foundation of arithmetic, language, history and science; for all intents and purposes I was prepared. I even looked like a teacher with my long skirt and gray vest. My room was filled with color, properly placed learning stations and opportunity for growth. I was ready, but of course I had no students.

The children finally arrived and, after a few weeks, the real work began. The challenges of making the lessons exciting and interesting was constantly in my forethoughts. I needed to not only teach and assess a lesson, but also reach the individualized learning style of every student. Their educational needs, abilities and disabilities were now becoming evident. The social interactions created a myriad of behavior struggles. I shared with parents my growing concerns. I was expected to educate, teach character, skill socially and train these young ones for life. Did I mention the paperwork? Ugh! I needed an extra six hours a day to keep up with the grading and planning!

I was in the trenches of teaching. Yes, I was prepared. Yes, I was right where God wanted me. Yes, I was a gifted teacher and would be successful. Yes, the children would learn in spite of my inadequacies. Yes, I was incredibly overwhelmed for I was in the battlefield of the classroom. I see you in a similar place, my dear Soldiers.

We are dressed in the full armor of God. *Now what?* We opened our eyes to the enemy of our souls that we battle against. We realized we needed God's perfectly designed armor on every day to live victoriously. We put on truth and righteousness through Christ. We placed shoes of peace on our feet and danced in His presence. *Now what?* We took faith and learned how to use it as a shield against the darts the enemy sends our way. We took the salvation of our past and placed it like a helmet over our minds to stay focused on God and all He has for us in the future. Eagerly, we accepted the sword of the Spirit, which is the Word of God, and have learned how to handle it expertly. Our full armor is a perfect fit, designed especially for us. *Now what?*

The enemy sends his lies, we battle in our mind and decide what to do. It is our military headquarters, of sorts. Then, we listen to our Commander and Chief, through His Word, our Sword of the Spirit. We surrender our all to Him. Trusting Him. We communicate with God through prayer. He listens and we trust His leadership.

Dressed in the armor, what is the *first thing* we do according to Ephesians 6:18?

Now what? The battle for our minds, souls, lives, families, and abundant life is fought in prayer. Prayer is the battlefield, and it is hard work.

In my mind, I battle with personal thoughts, self-talk, often lies of the enemy, and struggle with my thinking process, emotions and decisions. Satan tempts me and then I think about the temptation again and again. I continue to loop the same defeating thought over and over. Sometimes, I *yield* to it. But, when I stop to realize that God has a better plan, and contemplate His best for me, I immediately turn my thoughts and will to Him. I begin to communicate with God about my ways. I pray. I have given God the foothold in the battlefield for my mind, instead of Satan as mentioned in Ephesians 4:27. God moves on my behalf.

Give God the foothold.

Prayer places that battle to the Lord with a victory already won on the cross. Jesus died once for the sins of all, yours and mine. He already died for my selfish thoughts, my lies, my impatience, arrogance and whatever sinful thoughts that enter my mind. What kind of sinful thoughts and temptations enter your mind? How about a temptation to exaggerate a bit to make yourself sound better? (lie) Or what about thinking down about someone else? Perhaps judging them? (pride) You get the idea… ALL SINS. The battle has been won. Why do you think we strive to handle things ourselves and not surrender them in prayer to a mighty God? Why do we choose to fight the Spiritual battles brought our way without our Commander-in-Chief by our side to guide us? Why? (Yes, I'm waiting for an answer.)

 Let's answer some basic questions about prayer. **What? Where? Who? When? Why?**

What? Prayer is simply communicating with God and seeking His will.
Read Revelation 4:1-2 to see **where** this battle is fought.

What did John see?   What did John hear?   What did the voice say?

In Heaven, there is a THRONE ROOM.
Where is Jesus in the Throne Room?

Are we invited to go there? Read Hebrews 4:16.
How are we to come?   Why are we to come?

According to Hebrews 10:19, why are we permitted to enter the Holy Throne Room?

When I begin to pray I often picture myself entering the Holy Throne Room. I gather around the Throne of Grace. It is as beautiful as my limited, earthly imagination can make it.

Read Romans 8:26-27. Who is the subject of verse 26?   Verse 27?

Who "searches the heart", "knows the mind of the Spirit", and "makes intercession for the saints?"

 Reread Hebrews 4:16, this time including verse fifteen. Who is our High Priest?
With this in mind, read Hebrews 7:24-25. Why does Jesus, our High Priest, "ever-live?"

What does that mean to you?

What about the Spirit? Ephesians 6:18. We are told to pray "in the Spirit." He is there. The very moment we begin to pray, both Jesus and the Holy Spirit join us. It is never a *solo* of my heart to God, but rather a trio in three-part harmony pleading with the Father on my behalf. Once we give the Holy Spirit control of our lives, our communication with our Commander and Chief becomes the central focus in our distracted and busy lives.

What is the *second word* in Ephesians 6:18?   (This word *always* brings me conviction.)

What and **when** are we doing in Ephesians 5:20? When?
Philippians 1:4   Colossians 1:3   1 Thessalonians 5:17   Philemon 4

All things are possible with those who believe and that includes obedience to God's Word—*always*. I love the way J. Gordon Henry states it, "As the Holy Spirit moves we become so intimate with God that we will seldom pass through an experience before we speak to Him about it, either in supplication, in sighing, in pouring out our woes before Him, in fervent request, or in thanksgiving and adoration." This is "all prayers and supplication".

Our **why** is given in Jeremiah 33:3 says, *"Call to me and I will answer you and show you great and mighty things which you do not know."* He will show us. He will.

Many of us know Jeremiah 29:11, *"For I know the thoughts that I think toward you, says the Lord, thoughts of peace and not of evil, to give you a future and a hope."*
But what about the following verse in Jeremiah 29:12? What are we told to do in verse 12?

And what in that same verse will God do?

Say that aloud a couple times until you believe it as truth. Whether we truly believe it or not, it is truth. I'm speechless at the thought of God listening to me. ME? With all my flaws, sin, good intentions, and not-God-honoring thoughts? He listens.

 Sharpen Your Sword for Week Nine by writing and communicating your prayer requests.

 Write Ephesians 6:18.

The Perfect Fit

Week Nine   Day Two

Being Watchful

"...Praying always with all prayer and supplication in the Spirit, being watchful to this end with all perseverance and supplication for all the saints..." Ephesians 6:18

I love my dog! She is a mutt, part husky–part shepherd, and she brings me such joy. The family has decided that I am her favorite because her tail wags harder and she whines louder when she is expecting me. It is wonderful to be someone's favorite. Her name is Autumn.

Autumn is quite *watchful,* but not in the way we had hoped and planned. If a robber came to our door and entered, I'm confident that Autumn would greet him with tail wagging and then *watch* him rob us blind. She doesn't bark either. So much for hoping an intruder would be intimidated by the ferocious dog on the other side of the door. We hear her rushing to the window and that is the only warning you get that a stranger is around or a visitor has entered our yard. No scary sounds. No sounds at all. So much for our plans!

She is incredibly watchful in other ways and I appreciate her attentiveness. She *watches* squirrels out the window. She *watches* me as I drive in the yard. She *watches* with expectancy for the reward of a dog treat. She *watches* while I cook and is ready for a tad of food to drop to the floor. She *watches* with magnificent intensity where her tennis ball is when we are playing catch. And, oh, how she *watches* me. Actually, her entire body is *watching,* down to the tip of her tail.

Autumn is quiet, intense and focused. How I would love that description to be of me. I long to be quiet, intense and focused on the things of God. Yes, I have learned many a spiritual lesson from my dog!

Think about the Roman soldier *watching* as he carried out his duties. Picture his face as he kept watch over a prisoner or watched the enemy line for war to begin or intensely fought for his cause. The word **watch** means to wait for, observe, spy, scope out, especially in order to see approaching danger and to warn those who are endangered.

As a soldier of the Lord, I need to be watchful in several ways. The first is to be attentive or watchful to my surroundings. It is keeping my heart and spiritual eyes open for what the Lord desires of me. I desire to be so watchful that I would pray more about situations and circumstances than talk about them. I want to observe, then *go to the Throne before I go to the phone*. Another very practical way to be watchful is to just stay alert while I pray. And, a third, is to be watchful in expectancy for the Lord's answer. I long to be waiting upon the Lord for His leading in allowing the Holy Spirit to speak to my heart. It is being watchful for the Lord to give direction and discernment regarding challenging situations or individuals. Being watchful is being focused and ready for His will.

> # Go to the Throne, before I go to the phone.

Read Psalm 123:1-2. Who is the servant watchful toward?
I cannot help but think of a servant just waiting on his master—ready for his call. Perhaps the master doesn't even have to speak, he just looks a certain way and the servant jumps to oblige. The servant is completely focused and watchful to the desires of his master, and ready to serve.

 Put yourself in the place of the disciples of Matthew 26:36-46.
What did Jesus ask in verse 38b?   What happened in verse 40?

What did Jesus ask in verse 41?   What happens in verse 42?

What reason did Christ give for this weakness according to verse 41?

What are we to watch and pray about in Mark 13:33-37?

As soldiers we are to *be watchful to this end (Eph 6:18)*. What benefit is it to us if we do? VICTORY! Victory from the strongholds of sin. Jesus says that we are to watch and pray so that we don't fall into temptation. Dressed in the armor of truth, peace, righteousness, faith, and salvation, with the Word of God at our disposal, *we can still fall*. We need the intimacy and grounding of prayer. We can stand ready, *but prayer is where we fight* and God fights for us. It is where we appropriate this armor and surrender all to God.

The matter of prayer takes diligence and discipline unlike anything this world knows.

We must *be watchful* of our prayer life. Protect it and claim it as ours as soldiers of God. Prayer is not just confined to the moments you give God, but prayer actually begins hours before when you decide to get to bed early so you can be up to pray. It takes discipline. It takes tenacity. It takes preparation. The prayer warrior must guard her time, plan her schedule, and be watchful for anything that might hinder prayer—like perhaps, herself. After all, Jesus said it best, "The spirit is willing, but the flesh is weak."

I am in good company when I recall that the disciples (Mathew 26:36-46) struggled with being watchful in prayer. Like me, they experienced the *drowsies*. I've learned one way to stay alert during prayer is to pray aloud. Just a whisper will do. Another way is to keep a journal and write as you pray. (As you have been doing with the *Sharpen Your Sword* pages.) The benefits of journaling are endless. Of course, the writing will assist your alertness, but the written document will prove again and again that God is faithful. You can have your journal to refer to God's goodness when you are getting discouraged.

And the final way to *watch and pray* is just to be full of faith, confident that He will hear and answer, trusting His way and waiting with expectancy to what He will do...being full of God-confidence. Philippians 1:3-7 is a passage with promise. What is Paul confident of in verse six?

Let's close today with a sharp sword, Jeremiah 33:3. Write it in the area beloww.

 How does that promise encourage you today? Be specific.

We pray. He answers. Then He shows us amazing things.

> **Prayer is where we fight.**

If we believe that truth to our deepest part, it must affect the *watchfulness* of our prayers. It has to. We will be serious about watching and praying, because we will be ready to be astonished by our Amazing God. We will be confident that He will answer. HE WILL.

Sometimes, even when we fully believe God answers our prayers, we slack in praying with *perseverance*. We pray diligently about a matter, and then when the answer does not come in our timing, we lose our determination and stop praying.

Is there a desire or prayer request that you have stopped faithfully praying about? Salvation of a loved one, perhaps? If Jesus were to come to you today, and promise to answer all the prayers you prayed to Him *last week*, would things look different? Did you pray last week for the salvation of your family members? For the healing of a friend? About the deepest desires of your heart? I was asked that question recently, and conviction flooded my heart. I had not. We need perseverance in our prayers. Don't give up or give in, rather press in with persistency.

> **If all the prayers that we prayed last week were answered, how would our lives be different?**

Like my sweet dog focuses passionately, ready with every bit of herself, so must we be watchful unto our Master. We must sit and wait expectedly for Him, persistently bringing to Him our heart's desires. We need to know our surroundings, be alert to His every move and confident that He will answer. HE WILL.

 With great anticipation and watchfulness, record your prayer requests on **Sharpen Your Swords for Week Nine**. Be sure to include a promise from today's lesson.

 Pray about your memorization of Ephesians 6:10-18 asking God to give you the strength to complete this work that He has begun in you.

The Perfect Fit

Week Nine   Day Three

Power Packed Prayers

" Praying always with all power and supplication in the Spirit, being watchful to this end with all perseverance and supplication for all the saints..." Ephesians 6:18

Let's play a game.

I'll give you a word and you write the first word that comes to your mind. Ready?

Salt & _____

Romeo & _____

Black & _____

Milk & _____

Spaghetti & _____

Prayer & _____

Did the last one stump you? I thought it might, but by the end of today's reading, let's see if you can fill in that blank.

We've discussed prayer in much detail this week—its purpose, methods and practicality. But may I suggest we add something to your prayer life that will give it the power of God?

 In Ephesians 6:10-18, Paul listed the pieces of our armor, but yet only one is a weapon.

Which one would that be?

What does 2 Corinthians 10:4 say about the weapons we have for spiritual warfare? (note the plural)

The other primary weapon is clearly stated in Ephesians 6:18. What is it?

In Beth Moore's book, Praying God's Word, she shares the Greek word for power as being the adjective form of the term dunamai meaning "to be able." She then goes on to state that we get our English word dynamite from this Greek word power. God has handed us two sticks of dynamite with which to demolish our strongholds: His Word and prayer. Moore says power is when we take our two primary sticks of dynamite–prayer and the Word–strap them together and ignite them with faith in what God says He can do.

Praying God's word is using His very thoughts to agree with Him about the situations in our lives.

> **Prayer-less lives are powerless lives, and prayerful lives are powerful lives.**

Prayer keeps us in constant communication with God, relying on Him for our every day. After all, prayer-less lives are powerless lives, and prayerful lives are powerful lives.

God desires us to walk in power, but even more I believe He desires us to walk in His presence. He wants us to be healed, but even more I believe He wants us to know the Healer. He desires that we understand truth, but more He wants us to walk with the Truth. He is so much more concerned about our character and relationship with Him than our circumstances. We must be entirely connected to Him and *praying always* does just that. It is not about the way we live but WHO we live for. It is not about doing something, but the SOMEONE we focus our lives on. It's all about HIM.

Let's look again at 2 Corinthians 10:3-5, and the passage "taking captive every thought to make it obedient to Christ?" While looking at the helmet of salvation, we determined it was in our minds where many a battle is decided. Our thoughts must be His thoughts. We must choose to think Christ's thoughts about our situations, relationships and circumstances. Where can we find Christ's thoughts but in His word.

When I think His thoughts, the Word, I not only find myself in communication with Him through prayer, but my mind begins to be retrained or renewed, as mentioned in Romans 12:2. I begin to think His thoughts about my situation, rather than my own. Your weekly discipline to *Sharpen Your Sword* by including verses beside your prayer request, is a fabulous start in praying *power packed prayers*. Don't get bogged down with trying to find a prayer procedure that fits, just let God's Word speak to you concerning your prayer requests.

Read Psalm 119:18. Write this verse as a prayer. (It is already in prayer form.)

It is as simple as restating God's truth to Him and in doing so we reaffirm our own faith.

Read 1 Chronicles 16:34. Restate this truth as a prayer from your heart.

We can use God's Word to ask Him for things we need.

Read Philippians 4:19. Simply state this verse as a prayer, asking for something you need.

We can also use God's Word to confess sin in our lives. Read Proverbs 8:13. Write a prayer.

 Record one of these prayers in **Sharpen Your Sword for Week Nine**.

One way to approach learning to pray God's Word is to start with Paul's prayers recorded in the epistles. Using phrases of scripture or swords, is a way to pray God's Word.

You could use: "*wisdom and power*" (Ephesians 1:18-19), "*strength in the inner man*" (Ephesians 3:16-19), "*discernment*" (Philippians 1:9-11), "*have knowledge of God's will*" (Colossians 1:9), "*a growing love for one another*" (Colossians 3:10-13), "*be worthy of their calling*" (2 Thessalonians 1:11-12), "*be comforted and established*" (2 Thessalonians 2:16-17), "*steadfast in their love for God*" (2 Thessalonians 3:5), "*live a quiet and peaceable life*" (1 Timothy 2:1-2), and "*recognize all they have in Christ*" (Philemon 6).

Recently, my husband and I have been walking through some very difficult days with one of our daughters. I have felt God's peace and presence, but have also been praying promises to reaffirm my faith. The story of Jairus, in Luke 8:41-56, has ministered to me many times. I have found myself praying parts of that story over and over again. For example, look at Luke 8:50.

> **The Spirit of God ... turns cowards into conquerors, chaos into calm, cries into comfort.**

What were Jesus' words to Jairus?

 How could this be written as a prayer? Try it out.

I do not want to be afraid of what could happen to her. I only want to believe every promise in the Word on our daughter's behalf. I am reminded of Jesus' words and His love. I am revitalized with the fact that He loves me passionately and wants me only to trust Him. I am meditating on His words and praying them back to Him. I can testify that this practice is very powerful and produces power packed prayers. Oh, how I desire to be a woman of prayer.

I'd like to end today with a quote from Beth Moore's book, <u>Living Free</u>.

"The Spirit of God released through our prayers and the prayers of others turns cowards into conquerors, chaos into calm, cries into comfort. The enemy knows the power of prayer. He's been watching it furiously for thousands of years. Abraham prayed..., Isaac prayed..., Jacob prayed. ... Moses left Pharaoh and prayed. ...So Moses prayed for the people. ...Manoah prayed to the Lord. ... Samson prayed. ...Hannah wept much and prayed. ...So David prayed. ...Elijah stepped forward and prayed. ...And Elisha prayed, 'O Lord.' ...After Job had prayed for his friends. ...And Hezekiah prayed to the Lord. ...Daniel got down on his knees and prayed. ...From inside the fish Jonah prayed. ...Very early in the morning, while it was still dark, Jesus got up, left the house and went off to a solitary place, where He prayed. ...Going a little farther, He fell with His face to the ground and prayed."

Oh, how I want to be in that list as a woman who prayed. How about you?

Jesus sought His Father God in prayer. Oh, how much more must I? I am absolutely hopeless to live the abundant life without prayer. The Sword is not to be used alone, Soldier Sis, we must use our weapon of prayer and allow God to work His will in our lives.

So let's try the game again.

Peanut Butter & _____

Ham & _____

Prayer & _____

 Review Ephesians 6:10-18. Try as much as you can from memory. Good for you, Sister!

The Perfect Fit

Week Nine   Day Four

Fully Dressed

"...and for me, that utterance may be given to me, that I may open my mouth boldly to make known the mystery of the gospel, for which I am an ambassador in chains; that in it I may speak boldly, as I ought to speak." Ephesians 6:19-20

*P*aul is nearing the end of this letter he has penned to the Ephesians and we are nearing the end of our time together. He has just shared an incredible analogy using the armor relating to how we are to live victoriously in Christ. As he writes, you know he is fully dressed in the armor. The proof is throughout the writings of all the epistles he wrote: Romans, I & II Corinthians, Galatians, Ephesians, Philippians, Colossians, I & II Thessalonians, I & II Timothy, Titus and Philemon. What an impact his writings can make on our lives because he walked in obedience to God's leading! We can trust his testimony.

Dressed in the full armor, take note at what Paul does as he finishes this letter. In Ephesians 6:19-20, he asks for specific prayer for himself. Prayer should be our first activity, after we are fully dressed in the armor, and Paul leads by example. Prayer is where we surrender situations over to the Lord and allow Him to fight them for us.

If you had been under house arrest for your faith, chained to a Roman soldier without privacy, freedom or rights, what is the first thing you would have asked others to pray for?

I'm with you, Sister. I probably would have asked for my freedom, clean clothes and a cheesesteak sub with fried onions, but, according to verse 19, what does Paul ask for?

Paul was a gifted orator, powerful writer, and a very well-educated man that could explain his views, but he knew *he* was not where the power would come. Because he was dressed in the armor, he knew that any power, strength, or miraculous happenings were only going to come when God was the source. Paul was a confident, strong man, but he knew he needed to speak with God-confidence. So, he prays for utterance from heaven to speak boldly of God's mysteries.

Did he have struggles? Oh, yes. Did he have reason to complain? He was in chains for his faith and had a thorn in the flesh—not to mention the shipwrecks, beatings, and jail time. Paul knew trials better than Job, yet he walked in the full armor of God, humbly leaning on his Creator for strength.

 Read 2 Corinthians 11:22-33. Write some trials Paul experienced and in what did he decided to boast?

Paul knew he needed to speak boldly and share what God had done in his life. If prison was his lot, then he wanted to be an outspoken testimony to the gospel of Jesus Christ as an "ambassador in chains." He didn't ask for the Ephesians to pray for his situation to change, just that God would use him in the middle of his plight. No matter the situation, he desired to boldly share his story. His Story. No one can refute your story. It is yours! Speak it boldly. Those around us desperately need the peace, grace, forgiveness and love of God for living abundantly today, defeating the enemy tomorrow and enjoying God's presence forever.

 Name a few people that you know need the gospel of Jesus?

When in the next week would you be able to speak boldly, tell your story, or share a testimony with one of them? Be specific.

> **We need the love of God for living abundantly today, defeating the enemy tomorrow and enjoying God's presence forever.**

In 2 Corinthians 12:1-6, Paul's personal testimony states that he somehow went into the third heaven and heard unspeakable things. Something to boast about? We would think so, but Paul refuses to boast. According to verse six, what would he be if he did "boast?"

To be sure that no one thought of him too highly, and take the attention off of his Lord, Paul goes on to discuss his "thorn in the flesh" in verses 7-10. We don't know what it was, but we know Paul finally learned to embrace it as God's plan for his life.

When and where is God's strength made perfect? (v. 9)

What then does Paul encourage us to "boast in?" (v. 9-10)

"For when I am weak, then I am strong." 2 Corinthians 12:10

This is the verse that wraps up the way Paul lived in the full armor of God. He chose to embrace his difficulties, boast of his vulnerabilities and surrender himself to the Lord. He testified of what the Lord was doing, all the while wearing truth, righteousness, peace, faith, salvation and the Word of God. He knew when fully surrendered, his God would fight the battles for him and make him strong.

Paul's personal prayer request also reminds me that it is God's will to recruit others to intercede for us. There have been times I have not asked fellow believers to pray for me because I felt my requests were not as worthy as theirs. For some reason, I believed a personal prayer request was selfish. How absurd! Paul gives testimony to the importance of sharing your needs with others. It is all part of God's plan. We soldiers need fellow soldiers in battle.

Go ahead, Sister. Speak boldly, as you ought to speak.

Share your prayer request from **Sharpen Your Sword for Week Nine** with a Soldier Sister. Give testimony to the scripture that you chose to encourage you.

On the next page, see if you are able to complete the review of Ephesians 6:10-20. (Before you write on it, why not make a few copies to help you study.) Don't get discouraged. If you know part of the passage – Celebrate!! That is more than you knew a few weeks ago. You are doing great!!!

Ephesians 6:10-20 (NKJV)

*[10] Finally, my brethren, be strong in the Lord
and in the power of His might.*

*[11] Put on the whole armor of God, that you may be able to stand
against the wiles of the devil.*

*[12] For we do not wrestle against flesh and blood, but against principalities, against powers,
against the rulers of the darkness of this age,
against spiritual hosts of wickedness in the heavenly places.*

*[13.] Therefore take up the whole armor of God,
that you may be able to withstand in the evil day, and having done all, to stand.*

*14. Stand therefore having girded your loins with truth
and having put on the breastplate of righteousness.*

*15 And having shod your feet with the preparation of the gospel of peace.
16 Above all, taking the shield of faith
with which you will be able to quench all the fiery darts of the wicked one.*

17 And take the helmet of salvation, and the sword of the Spirit, which is the word of God;

*18 praying always with all prayer and supplication in the Spirit,
being watchful to this end with all perseverance and supplication for all the saints –*

*19 and for me, that utterance may be given to me,
that I may open my mouth boldly to make known the mystery of the gospel,*

20 for which I am an ambassador in chains; that in it I may speak boldly, as I ought to speak

The Perfect Fit

Week Nine   Day Five

Wounded, Yet Still Fighting

"Do not be afraid, only believe, and she will be made well." Luke 8:50b

God is the Master Teacher and there was no way He was going to allow me to do a complete study of the full armor of God, without a final exam to see if I really comprehended what I had learned. As I was completing the study on prayer, a major life battle began and the enemy came in with arrows flying. War was declared! Each fiery dart was flaming with fear, disappointment, anger, bewilderment, confusion, discouragement, pride, rage, self-pity, shame and tons of worry.

As mothers, there is nothing that can challenge our faith like when our children are in life, and possibly death, situations. A few weeks ago our sixteen-year-old daughter found herself right smack in the middle of one. What began as a typical girl-teen struggle, turned into an addiction that left us, as parents, making decisions that seemed impossible to imagine. As the arrows came at us in every direction, I knew there was no way I could walk through this valley without my personalized, spiritual armor firmly in place. I very deliberately put it on, piece by piece by piece, with all intentions to not take it off for a moment. I was going to eat, sleep, work, rest, and walk fully dressed.

I knew our family was in God's hands and that this trial was permitted to come our way. I imagined our name being mentioned "in the heavenlies" and God saying that His strength would be made perfect in our weakness. I tried to pray before every encounter, knowing that in the Throne Room of prayer the battles are surrendered and fought by God Himself.

I put on my belt of truth, believing fully that God was in control even though life seemed to be spinning wildly out of control. I humbly put on God's breastplate of righteousness and prayed that His Spirit would work through me in the lives of others–especially, my daughter's. I wanted to be compassionate, kind, understanding, and firm, yet Christ-like in my every encounter. Those shoes of peace where firmly laced onto my feet and I was determined to only step where God directed.

I think of those initial days of the battle as *valley-days*. They were difficult, trying and challenging, yet revitalizing, life giving and full of faith. I walked through the valley determined to hang onto the truth that God was in control, His righteousness was mine and my feet were firmly planted on the rock. My shoes of peace were mud covered, because I refused to move off the Rock as the storm raged. The mud was actually coming up about my ankles. I felt the enemy's attempts to push me into one of the many pits that the valley holds. But I was resolute to not budge. Call me stubborn, but my mind was made up.

> **My shoes of peace were mud covered.**

The valley is a place of decision, because everywhere one turns there is opportunity to grow or not grow in faith. Those fiery darts of confusion and discouragement were constantly in my sight, on my mind and nearing my heart. I would gain victory over them by fighting with my spiritual armor, but then would have to decide what to do with the extinguished dart that lay beside me. Victory was mine, but the temptation to pick up that arrow and rehearse, review and n*urse it back to health* was a sad option. I knew *looping it* would not be beneficial for anyone. So, I decided to leave the now cold arrows, the broken pieces, for God to clean up. I just moved on to the next battle stronger than before.

While embracing the *valley-days,* I noticed the beauty of this time and place. The incredible LIFE that is evident in the valley—green grass, flowers, flowing water, *and growing-life* at every turn. I picked up my shield of faith and asked some to help me hold it high, to lift my arms when they became weary. I implored sisters and brothers of the faith, my fellow soldiers, to surround my daughter and our family in the tortoise formation. I put on my helmet of salvation, held my head high, and confidently trusted in my Father, the Creator of the Universe. He had all of these details in His hands. I would not be defeated by the strategies of the enemy! And then, I reached for the amazing Sword of the Spirit, the Word of God.

I had used the Sword before in life's battles, reading and memorizing it to strengthen me during difficult days. I had written passages out and held them in my pockets, posted them on my fridge, meditated on them over and over again, but this time the warfare seemed more intense than ever before. I felt the darkness and the arrows strike one after another. I knew, without a doubt, that the enemy was trying to steal the very life and future of my child. I knew this was a spiritual battle that could only be fought with spiritual warfare.

Scripture became my LIFE. I didn't have the luxury of time to sit and read it hours upon hours, but I did pick it up and FIGHT. Some of the swords I chose from the armory of the entire Word were familiar ones that were sharpened throughout this experience. Psalm 91 encouraged my heart over and over again.

Psalm 91:1-6
He who dwells in the secret place of the Most High
Shall abide under the shadow of the Almighty
I will say of the Lord, "He is my refuge and my fortress,
My God, in Him I will trust."
Surely He shall deliver you from the snare of the fowler,
And from the perilous pestilence,
He shall cover you with His feathers,
And under His wings you shall take refuge;
His truth shall be your shield and buckler,
You shall not be afraid of the terror by night,
Nor of the arrow that flies by day,
Nor of the pestilence that walks in darkness,
Nor of the destruction that lays waste at noonday.

Notice the many references to the enemy and his tactics. We are told to not be afraid because God chooses to honor and bless those who trust in Him. Go ahead and rejoice in how this blessed chapter concludes. (I'm changing the masculine to feminine so we can relate a little bit more intimately, Ladies.)

Psalm 91:14-16
Because she has set her love upon me, therefore I will deliver her;
I will set her on high, because she has known my name.
She shall call upon me, and I will answer her,
I will be with her in trouble,
I will deliver her and honor her.
With long life I will satisfy her,
And show her my salvation.

When this battle first began, and the arrows were targeting my heart, into my spirit God brought the story of Jairus' daughter from Luke 8:40-56. (We studied it together in Week Six about the shield of faith.) I read and reread this passage and every time I was amazed by Jesus' kindness in the words to Jairus, "Do not be afraid, only believe, and she will be made well." Those words, as well as many in this passage, encouraged me. I actually repeated those words aloud to the enemy on several occasions when fear, doubt and worry bullied their way into my life. I found myself putting those words into a prayer: "Lord, help me to not be afraid. Help me to only believe that she will be made well." And I always added the wording of verse 56, "Lord, astonish me!"

There were other passages that strengthened me and were effective as swords to defeat the enemy. Many scriptures reinforced the truth that God is in control and victory was only going to come with full surrender. Dressed in the armor, in the midst of this *valley* experience, God's word gave me the victory for most days.

Most days.

Not every day.

> **I knew I wasn't forsaken, but many tears were shed and my heart was broken.**

Were there days when I was tired? Weary? Too exhausted of fighting this spiritual and physical warfare to continue on full force? You better believe it.

We are only human. We get weary. That's why Jesus says, "Come to Me, all who are weary and heavy-laden and I will give you rest." (Matthew 11:28) Very honestly, there were certain days and specific situations that were overwhelming for me, even fully dressed in the armor. I was not defeated, but surely felt hard-pressed and perplexed. I was reminded of Paul's writings to the Corinthians.

 Read 2 Corinthians 4:7-15. Write down your thoughts on this passage.

I knew I wasn't forsaken, but many tears were shed and my heart broken. Many tears.

Psalm 56:8 (NLT)–You keep track of all my sorrows. You have collected all my tears in your bottle. You have recorded each one in your book. Not a tear was wasted. Each silent tear was a prayer to God that He heard, collected, recorded and felt. Every single tear.

I recall one particular therapy session in which I sat, tear-filled tissue in hand, anxiously waiting to get out so I could cry hard to my God. I so wanted to put my shield and sword down long enough to wrap my empty arms around my Savior's neck. I was ready to weep on His Almighty shoulder and just have Him hold me like He had so many times before. I was one weary soldier. I left that session, went for a walk by myself and wailed

> **Each silent tear was a prayer to God that He heard, collected, recorded and felt.**

loudly. Honestly, it was the hardest I had ever cried in my entire life. I talked passionately to my God. I needed to tell Him my deepest hurts. I knew only He would want to hear them all. After weeping for a bit, I felt refreshed, *ready to pick up my shield and sword and enter back into the battle.* We cannot stay too long undressed.

Psalm 126:5-6
Those who sow in tears,
Shall reap in joy.
He who continually goes forth weeping,
Bearing seed for sowing,
Shall doubtless come again with rejoicing,
Bringing his sheaves with him.

I had hope and chose again not to lose heart. I was reminded that He was working all this out for my good—and for our daughter's good. I could not physically see the enemy about me, but I felt the terrible sting of his arrows. They were real. And so was the glorious spiritual shield Jesus holds to protect me.

 I clung to 2 Corinthians 4:16-18. How do the "light afflictions" compare to the "exceeding and eternal weight of glory?"

The following song, by Twila Paris, has been my theme song.
Find it, listen, put down your shield and worship.

The Warrior Is a Child
By Twila Paris

Lately I've been winning battles left and right
But even winners can get wounded in the fight.
People say that I'm amazing, strong beyond my years.
But they don't see inside of me, I'm hiding all the tears.

They don't know, that I go running home when I fall down
They don't know who picks me up when no one is around
I drop my sword and cry for just a while
'Cause deep inside this armor, The warrior is a child

Unafraid because His armor is the best
But even soldiers need a quiet place to rest
People say that I'm amazing, never face retreat
But they don't see the enemies that lay me at His feet

 Write your final request on **Sharpen Your Sword for Week Nine**. Share a verse to pray.

 Feeling weary? Put your shield down and rest in the treasure you have memorized in Ephesians 6:10-20.

The Perfect Fit

Week Nine   Bonus

Dancing in My Perfectly Fitted Armor

"Finally, my brethren, be strong in the Lord and in the power of His might. Put on the whole armor of God, that you may be able to stand against the wiles of the devil." Ephesians 6:10-22

We started <u>The Perfect Fit</u> with the word *finally,* and now it *finally* fits. During each week the actual Roman soldier's piece was detailed, practical application was offered and then closed with what **my** personalized armor of God looked like in my mind. Each piece of the armor carries its intended spiritual application, but how I view myself in God's magnificent plan wearing it, is what I have intended to share.

I see myself as a woman of God, fully dressed in the armor – gracefully dancing in freedom, living abundantly in full surrender to my Lord. Yes, my armor represents an elegant dancer–gliding, sashaying and worshiping – full of praise.

My whole armor of God is not bulky, awkward and uncomfortable, but rather is stunning, form-fitting and flattering. The first piece, my belt of truth, is a flowing, gold ribbon. Gold is a metal of high value, practical and beautiful. God's truth is practical, of the highest value and we see His beauty in it. Our second piece, my breastplate of righteousness, is a glistening white gown that reflects Christ and His righteousness when I live in a way that honors Him. The third piece of the armor I keep on are my shoes of peace. They are soft, pink ballet slippers that lace up, ever so elegantly, so I can stand without slipping. They support me in my every step and I walk sure-footedly. Yes, I dance freely. Light on my feet.

Next, are the pieces of armor with which I dance. My shield of faith, although covered with dings and dents as reminders of past victories, is held high to quench the fiery darts the enemy sends my way. I have learned to dance and live abundantly while strategically warding off the enemies schemes. This is made possible because my mind is stayed on Christ while I am wearing the helmet of salvation... my tiara. It keeps me focused on what Christ has done, is doing and will be doing on my behalf. I strive to think as He does. The final, and only offensive weapon I carry, is the sword of the Spirit, which is the Word of God. The sword cannot be softened, but is sharpened by my daily use of it. I become a better swordsman, knowing how to fight the battles of life using the Word of God. It sharpens me so I know God's heart and what pleases Him. My worship is sincere.

Once dressed, what is the first thing I do? I surrender my will to my Father God. I pray, "Your will, not mine, be done." I walk in complete submission to the God that provided such radiant armor. I pray to God, my God, that has a hope and future planned out for me. I pray.

I communicate with God, seeking His will, and surrendering situations, trials, struggles and tribulations over to Him. I embrace the fact that He has allowed them into my life, and trust Him to fight the battles for me. I know that the battle is the Lord's. I walk in faith trusting my Commander-in-Chief.

In my armor, I'm fully dressed for victory and filled with the Holy Spirit. Fully aware of the presence of God's Spirit, I'm dressed for abundant life on this earth and heaven, too. I'm free in Christ to worship and live as a daughter of God. I am strong in the Lord and in the power of His might. When I put on the whole armor of God, I stand. When I am so secure in Christ, I not only stand, I dance.

I can appreciate that dancing with excellence takes stamina, energy, concentration and practice. It includes my heart being in the right place with others and my God. My sins are forgiven. I am holding no bitterness toward anyone and I am full of the peace of God. Otherwise, my dancing would not be as elegant, graceful, or free from stumbling.

Could I dance and live free in Christ, fully dressed in my *spiritual* armor while carrying the weights and cares of this world? Does the armor fit me perfectly when I am upset with my sister? If I am *at odds* with another, can I wear the breastplate of righteousness? When I am worried, stressed and afraid, am I equipped to use my shield of faith? When I am gossiping and telling everyone my troubles, instead of seeking the Lord in prayer about a situation, am I allowing God to fight the battles for me?

I cannot worship when I am carrying burdens, fretting about the world, and bitter toward another. Can you imagine a trained ballet dancer with a heavy weight on her back, bundles of bags in her right hand and over-stuffed luggage in her left? Even the most excellent artist would trip over herself with such baggage. We need to be free of care.

Recently, this lesson was brought home to me as I sat awaiting the admission of our daughter into a rehab facility. Fearful thoughts, detailed concerns, fiery darts and a broken heart flooded my thinking. I looked at my surroundings, swallowed hard, and continued praying for God to intervene. He spoke to my spirit and asked, "How can you pick up your sword and shield with your arms full?" I looked at my empty hands, and contemplated His question. Noting my confusion, he added, "Your hands are full... of your daughter. Surrender her to me."

I understood. I couldn't use my hands to maneuver my shield and pick up my sword when they were full of my precious daughter. I needed to trust God's direction. At that moment, I surrendered her again to her Creator. I placed my daughter into the arms of the Great Physician. I gave up fighting myself and allowed Him to fight this battle for me. My hands were free to fight the enemy and dance in the Light. I could work, worship, live and dance in complete freedom. It felt and feels astonishingly exhilarating. I call it abundant life.

 In closing, let's consider the beautiful simplicity of Christ's words in John 10:10.
"The thief does not come except to steal, and to kill, and to destroy,
I have come that they may have life, and that they may have it more abundantly."

How does wearing the whole armor of God prepare us for the tactics of the thief?

How does wearing the whole armor of God provide access to abundant life?

What does your armor look like?

Are you free, in Christ, to wear it and use it to fight the arrows that come your way?

That's power… the power of His might. In it we can stand, walk, skip, hop and even dance. We quench fiery darts, persistently pray and speak boldly, as we ought to speak.

I realize I cannot *speak boldly* until I am fully dressed in my spiritual armor. Am I perfect? Far from it. But, I am a work in progress and miraculously God uses me. Everyday.

I am His.   He is mine.   Completely.   Surrendered.

He leads in all His magnificent glory. I follow in my armor. We dance together.

The Perfect Fit

Sharpen Your Sword

Week Nine

Concern	Truth to Believe	Date	Answer
A worry	Proverbs 3:5-6 "He will direct my paths."		

The Perfect Fit

Week Nine Wrap Up

Principal Questions for Week Nine

1. Describe the spiritual battle fought in Revelation 4:1-2.

2. Put yourself in the place of the disciples of Matthew 26:36-46.

What did Jesus ask in verse 38b?

What happened in verse 40?

What did Jesus ask in verse 41?

What happens in verse 42?

What reason did Christ give for this weakness according to verse 41?

3. Compare the 'weapons' mentioned in Ephesians 6:10-18 and 2 Corinthians 10:4.

4. Read 2 Corinthians 11:22-33 and think about Paul's trials yet what did he boast of?

5. Write your thoughts about 2 Corinthians 4:7-15.

Bonus. Consider the simplicity of Jesus' words in John 10:10; who is the thief?

Practical Questions for Week Nine

1. Why is the immortality of Jesus in Hebrews 7:24-25 important to you?

2. How does the promise written in Jeremiah 33:3 encourage you?

3. Write Luke 8:50 as a prayer.

4. If you were in Paul's situation in Ephesians 6:19, what is the first thing you would have asked others to pray for?

5. Think about 2 Corinthians 4:16-18; why does Paul compare 'light afflictions' to the 'exceeding and eternal weight of glory?'

Bonus. Think about and describe your personal suit of armor.

The Perfect Fit

A few Swords from the Armory concerning:
WORRY   FEAR   ANXIOUSNESS

Deuteronomy 31:6

Be strong and of good courage, do not fear nor be afraid of them; for the LORD your God, He is the One who goes with you. He will not leave you nor forsake you. (NKJV)

Joshua 1:3-9 selections

For I will be with you as I was with Moses. I will not fail you or abandon you.

Be strong and courageous. Be strong and very courageous. Be careful to obey all the instructions Moses gave you. Do not deviate from them, turning either to the right or to the left. Then you will be successful in everything you do. Study this Book of Instruction continually. Meditate on it day and night so you will be sure to obey everything written in it. Only then will you prosper and succeed in all you do. This is my command—be strong and courageous! Do not be afraid or discouraged. For the Lord your God is with you wherever you go. (NLT)

1 Chronicles 28:20

David also said to Solomon his son, "Be strong and courageous, and do the work. Do not be afraid or discouraged, for the LORD God, my God, is with you. He will not fail you or forsake you until all the work for the service of the temple of the LORD is finished. (NIV)

Psalm 27:1

The LORD is my light and my salvation; Whom shall I fear? The LORD is the strength of my life; Of whom shall I be afraid? (KJV)

Psalm 56:3

When I am afraid, I will trust in you. In God, whose word I praise, in God I trust; I will not be afraid. What can mortal man do to me? (NIV)

Isaiah 41:1

So do not fear, for I am with you; do not be dismayed, for I am your God. I will strengthen you and help you; I will uphold you with my righteous right hand. (NIV)

Isaiah 41:13

For I am the LORD, your God, who takes hold of your right hand and says to you, Do not fear; I will help you. (NIV)

Matthew 10:26

Therefore do not fear them. For there is nothing covered that will not be revealed, and hidden that will not be known. (NKJV)

Romans 8:15

For ye have not received the spirit of bondage again to fear; but ye have received the Spirit of adoption, whereby we cry, Abba, Father. (KJV)

1 Corinthians 16:13

Be on your guard; stand firm in the faith; be men of courage; be strong. (NIV)

2 Timothy 1:7

For God has not given us a spirit of fear and timidity, but of power, love, and self-discipline. (NLT)

Hebrews 13:5-6

For He Himself has said, "I will never leave you nor forsake you." So we may boldly say: "The LORD is my helper; I will not fear. What can man do to me?" (NKJV)

1 Peter 3:13-14

Who is going to harm you if you are eager to do good? But even if you should suffer for what is right, you are blessed. "Do not fear what they fear; do not be frightened." (NIV)

1 John 4:18

There is no fear in love. But perfect love drives out fear, because fear has to do with punishment. The one who fears is not made perfect in love. (NIV)

A few Swords from the Armory for when you are:
HURTING

Psalms 9:9

The LORD is a shelter for the oppressed and a refuge in times of trouble. (NLT)

Psalms 27:4-5

One thing have I asked of the LORD, that will I seek after: that I may dwell in the house of the LORD all the days of my life, to gaze upon the beauty of the LORD and to inquire in his temple. For he will hide me in his shelter in the day of trouble; he will conceal me under the cover of his tent; he will lift me high upon a rock. (NIV)

Psalms 46:1

God is our refuge and strength, a ever present help in trouble. (NIV)

1 Peter 5:6-7

Humble yourselves therefore under the mighty hand of God, that he may exalt you in due time: Casting all your care upon him; for he careth for you. (KJV)

Psalms 22:24

For he has not despised or abhorred the affliction of the afflicted, nor has he hidden his face from him, but when he cried to him he heard. (NKJV)

Psalms 56:8

You number my wanderings; put my tears into your bottle. Are they are not in your book? (NKJV)

Psalms 116:1-2

I love the LORD, for he heard my voice; He heard my cry for mercy. Because he turned his ear to me, I will call on him as long as I live. (NIV)

Jeremiah 29:11

For I know the thoughts that I think toward you, saith the LORD, thoughts of peace, and not of evil, to give you an expected end. (KJV)

A few Swords from the Armory for when you are praying over:

FINANCES

Matthew 6:24

No one can serve two masters. Either he will hate the one and love the other, or he will be devoted to the one and despise the other. You cannot serve both God and Money. (NIV)

Mark 4:19

But the worries of this life, the deceitfulness of wealth and the desires for other things come in and choke the word, making it unfruitful. (NIV)

Proverbs 23:4-5

Do not wear yourself out to get rich; do not trust your own cleverness. Cast but a glance at riches, and they are gone, for they will surely sprout wings and fly off to the sky like an eagle. (NIV)

Proverbs 11:28

He who trusts in his riches will fall, but the righteous shall flourish as the green leaf. (NIV)

Luke 8:14

The seed that fell among thorns stands for those who hear, but as they go on their way they are choked by life's worries, riches and pleasures, and they do not mature. (NIV)

Ecclesiastes 5:10

Whoever loves money never has enough; whoever loves wealth is never satisfied with their income. This too is meaningless. (NIV)

Proverbs 11:4

Wealth is worthless in the day of wrath, but righteousness delivers from death. (NIV)

Psalm 62:10

..if riches increase, do not set your heart on them (NIV)

2 Cor. 12:9-10

"But He has said to me, "My grace is sufficient for you, for my power is perfected in weakness" ... Therefore I am well content with weaknesses, with insults, with distresses, with persecutions, with difficulties, for Christ's sake; for when I am weak, then I am strong." (NIV)

Romans 8:28

And we know that in all things God works for the good of those who love him, who have been called according to his purpose. (NIV)

The Perfect Fit

A few Swords from the Armory for when you are praying for:

HOPE   PEACE   COURAGE   FAITH

Psalm 138:3

In the day when I cried out, You answered me, and made me bold with strength in my soul. (NKJV)

Matthew 19:26

Jesus looked at them and said to them, 'With men this is impossible, but with God all things are possible. (NIV)

2 Corinthians 4:16

Therefore we do not lose heart. Even though our outward man is perishing, yet the inward man is being renewed day by day. (NKJV)

Philippians 4:13

I can do all things through Christ who strengthens me. (NKJV)

John 16:33

I have told you these things, so that in me you may have peace. In this world you will have trouble. But take heart! I have overcome the world. (NIV)

Colossians 3:15

And let the peace that comes from Christ rule in your hearts. For as members of one body you are called to live in peace. And always be thankful. (NLT)

Psalms 46:1

God is our refuge and strength, an ever-present help in trouble. (NIV)

John 14:27

Peace I leave with you; my peace I give you. I do not give to you as the world gives. Do not let your hearts be troubled and do not be afraid. (NIV)

Numbers 6:26

The Lord turn his face toward you and give you peace. (NIV)

Psalm 29:11

The Lord gives strength to his people. The Lord blesses his people with peace. (NIV)

Philippians 4:6-7

Do not be anxious about anything, but in everything, by prayer and petition, with thanksgiving, present your requests to God. And the peace of God, which transcends all understanding, will guard your hearts and your minds in Christ Jesus. (NIV)

Romans 5:1

Therefore, since we have been made right in God's sight by faith, we have peace with God because of what Jesus Christ our Lord has done for us. (NLT)

Romans 15:13

Now may the God of hope fill you with all joy and peace in believing, so that you will abound in hope by the power of the Holy Spirit. (NASV)

John 14:1-3

Do not let your hearts be troubled. Trust in God; trust also in me. In my Father's house are many rooms; if it were not so, I would have told you. I am going there to prepare a place for you. And if I go and prepare a place for you, I will come back and take you to be with me that you also may be where I am. (NIV)

Psalm 55:22

Cast your burden on the Lord, and he shall sustain you: and he shall never permit the righteous to be moved. (NKJV)

Ecclesiastes 3:11

He has made everything beautiful in its time. He has also set eternity in the hearts of men; yet they cannot fathom what God has done from beginning to end. (NIV)

2 Thessalonians 3:16

Now may the Lord of peace himself give you peace at all times and in every way. The Lord be with all of you. (NIV)

A few Swords from the Armory for when you are praying for:

HEALING

Isaiah 41:10

So do not fear, for I am with you; do not be dismayed, for I am your God. I will strengthen you and help you; I will uphold you with my righteous right hand. (NIV)

James 5:14

Is anyone among you sick? Let them call the elders of the church to pray over them and anoint them with oil in the name of the Lord. (NIV)

Matthew 11:28

"Come to me, all you who are weary and burdened, and I will give you rest." (NIV)

Philippians 4:19

And my God will meet all your needs according to the riches of his glory in Christ Jesus. (NIV)

Proverbs 4:20-22

My son, pay attention to what I say; turn your ear to my words. Do not let them out of your sight, keep them within your heart; for they are life to those who find them and health to one's whole body. (NIV)

Exodus 15:26

He said, "If you listen carefully to the LORD your God and do what is right in his eyes, if you pay attention to his commands and keep all his decrees, I will not bring on you any of the diseases I brought on the Egyptians, for I am the LORD, who heals you." (NIV)

Mark 5:34

He said to her, "Daughter, your faith has healed you. Go in peace and be freed from your suffering." (NIV)

The Perfect Fit

A few Swords from the Armory for when you are praying about:

ADDICTION STRUGGLE DEFEAT SIN

1 Corinthians 10:13-14

No temptation has overtaken you except what is common to mankind. And God is faithful; he will not let you be tempted beyond what you can bear. But when you are tempted, he will also provide a way out so that you can endure it. Therefore, my dear friends, flee from idolatry. (NIV)

I John 2:16

For everything in the world – the lust of the flesh, the lust of the eyes, and the pride of life – comes not from the Father but from the world. (NIV)

I Corinthians 15:33

Do not be misled: "Bad company corrupts good character."(NIV)

James 4:7

Submit yourselves, then, to God. Resist the devil, and he will flee from you. (NIV)

I Corinthians 6:12

"I have the right to do anything," you say – but not everything is beneficial. "I have the right to do anything" – but I will not be mastered by anything." (NIV)

I Peter 5:10

And the God of all grace, who called you to his eternal glory in Christ, after you have suffered a little while, will himself restore you and make you strong, firm and steadfast. (NIV)

Psalm 50:15

And call on me in the day of trouble; I will deliver you, and you will honor me. (NIV)

Romans 5:3-5

Not only so, but we also glory in our sufferings, because we know that suffering produces perseverance; perseverance, character; and character, hope. And hope does not put us to shame, because God's love has been poured out into our hearts through the Holy Spirit, who has been given to us. (NIV)

I Corinthians 6:9-11

Or do you not know that wrongdoers will not inherit the kingdom of God? Do not be deceived: Neither the sexually immoral nor idolaters nor adulterers nor men who have sex with men 10 nor thieves nor the greedy nor drunkards nor slanderers nor swindlers will inherit the kingdom of God. 11 And that is what some of you were. But you were washed, you were sanctified, you were justified in the name of the Lord Jesus Christ and by the Spirit of our God. (NIV)

Titus 2:12

It teaches us to say, "No" to ungodliness and worldly passions, and to live self-controlled, upright and godly lives in this present age. (NIV)

James 1:2-3

Consider it pure joy, my brothers and sisters, whenever you face trials of many kinds, because you know that the testing of your faith produces perseverance. (NIV)

Hebrews 4:15-16

For we do not have a high priest who is unable to empathize with our weaknesses, but we have one who has been tempted in every way, just as we are – yet he did not sin. Let us then approach God's throne of grace with confidence, so that we may receive mercy and find grace to help us in our time of need. (NIV)

John 3:16-17

For God so loved the world that he gave his one and only Son, that whoever believes in him shall not perish but have eternal life. 17 For God did not send his Son into the world to condemn the world, but to save the world through him. (NIV)

Philippians 4:13

I can do all this through him who gives me strength. (NIV)

Matthew 6:13

And lead us not into temptation, but deliver us from the evil one. (NIV)

Matthew 26:41

Watch and pray so that you will not fall into temptation. The spirit is willing, but the flesh is weak. (NIV)

NLT – New Living Translation

NKJV – New King James Version

KJV – King James Version

NIV – New International Version

The Perfect Fit

A Few Favorite Swords from the Armory

(Record your favorite swords/verses to use in battle.)

Endnotes

Week Three Day Two 1. Tim Greenwood, "The Whole Armor of God," 11-19-99, www.tgm.org/aog-WholeArmor.htm.

Week Three Day Three 1. Henry, J Gordon, "Spiritual Warfare," J. Gordon Henry, Murfreesboro, TN, 1996.

Week Four Day One 1. Tim Greenwood, "The Whole Armor of God," 11-19-99, www.tgm.org/aog-WholeArmor.htm.

2. Tim Greenwood, "The Whole Armor of God," 11-19-99, www.tgm.org/aogWholeArmor.htm.

Week Five Day One 1. RW Research, Inc, The Armor of God, Rose Publishing, Torrance, California, 2005.

2. Tim Greenwood, "The Whole Armor of God," 11-19-99, www.tgm.org/aogWholeArmor.htm.

Week Five Day Four 1. Henry, J Gordon, "Spiritual Warfare," J. Gordon Henry, Murfreesboro, TN, 1996.

Week Six Day One 1. Tim Greenwood, "The Whole Armor of God," 11-19-99, www.tgm.org/aog-WholeArmor.htm.

Week Six Day Two 1. Henry, J Gordon, "Spiritual Warfare," J. Gordon Henry, Murfreesboro, TN, 1996.

Week Six Day Five 1. RW Research, Inc., The Armor of God, Rose Publishing, Torrance, California, 2005.

Week Seven Day One 1. Tim Greenwood, "The Whole Armor of God," 11-19-99, www.tgm.org/aogWholeArmor.htm.

2. Henry, J Gordon, "Spiritual Warfare," J. Gordon Henry, Murfreesboro, TN, 1996.

Week Eight Day One 1. Henry, J Gordon, Spiritual Warfare, J. Gordon Henry, Murfreesboro, TN, 1996.

2. Bishop Paul Hinder, Holy Spirit Interactive, Copyright © 2004-2012, www.holyspiritinteractive.net

Week Eight Day Four 1. Radmacher, E. D. The Nelson Study Bible: New King James Version. Includes index. (Ps 119:1). T. Nelson Publishers: Nashville,1997.

Suggested Answers to the Weekly Sessions

The Perfect Fit

Session #1 – foundation; prisoner; blessed; alive; mystery; gifts; out with the old; relationships

Session #2 – battlefield; enemy; person or situation; Satan; enemy; defend; offensive; been defeated

Session #3 – mind; walk in the flesh; mighty; thought; authority; us; Dig Deep; Repent; Embrace; Stand; Stumble; (your suggestion); to deceive; be real; Jesus; God has spoken

Session #4 – (your suggestion – morally right living); Imputed; justified; reminding; righteousness in Christ; Un-forgiveness; Imparted; reflecting; Holy Living; Holy Spirit; Jesus

Session #5 – (your suggestion); with; of; peaceful; our decision; Jesus; Blessed; alive; mystery; gifts; out with the old; relationships; God has spoken; Holy Living; Peace-filled walk

Session #6 – (your suggestion); salvation; believe; Shield; shield; (Following are suggestions only) Contentment; Rest; Peace; Putting Up with Others; Being Considerate; Confidence & Strength; Patience; Pure Thoughts; Confidentiality; God's Forgiveness; Love/Faith; Truth; Songs of Praise

Session #7 – mind; choice; battle; fought (it is fought in prayer); mind of Christ; truth; righteousness; peace; faith; salvation; God's Word

Session #8 – alive; unbeliever; Word; The Word of God; defeat the enemy

Session #9 – Throne Room; Father; works; prayerlessness; breathing; adoration; confession; thanksgiving; supplication; Holy Spirit and Jesus; diligent; casualties of war

Some testimonials

"Mona is a gifted teacher and speaker with a heart for women. She inspires, encourages, and challenges women with solid Bible teaching, insightful object lessons and personal stories. Her passionate love for the Lord, for His Word and for women is contagious and her powerful teaching is life changing."

Pastor J. Hartman Baltimore, MD

"The Perfect Fit seminar was edifying and encouraging as Mona related the scriptures of Ephesians 6 to a woman's everyday life. Her lovely signing enhanced the ministry of the way she presented God's Word."

Carol S. Afton, NY

"We were blessed to have Mona as our weekend speaker for our Ladies Retreat. Mona has a heart for God which spills over as she shares with women. God has blessed her with a unique way of connecting with women and talking about the issues that are relevant to women. We loved having her!"

Vonnie A Pinebrook Bible Conference, Stroudsburg, PA

"Mona brings so much encouragement to the lives of women. We thank God for her allowing God's Spirit to shine through and into the hearts of others. We are looking forward to having her back again."

Melissa, a mom from Camp Hebron Millersville, PA

"For our banquet Mona built her message around our theme "Recipes". She showed us what spiritual ingredients we need in our everyday lives to be more like Jesus. Her creative visual aids made it a night of fun with teaching that gets to your heart! She is a Godly woman that reaches both the young and old with illustrations that you will never forget. I want to hear her teaching again."

Judy H. Harrisonville, NJ

Many women have completed "The Perfect Fit – A Woman's Look at the Armor of God" and this is what they had to say:

"The Perfect Fit, was a perfect fit for me. I enjoyed how it tied the many Bible stories to the pieces of Armor showing me in so many ways how I could apply that to my life. It is also a joy to be taught by a teacher who also wears the armor by the way she lives."

Carolyn D.   Elmer, NJ

"The Perfect Fit is a timely study filled with Truth, Promise, Blessings and a blueprint for Victory. 'Obedience to get dressed leads to the anointing by God and His promise over flowing not only for us, but also for our generations to come.' When we put on our armor our children benefit".

Lucy K.   Toms River, NJ

"I have heard many messages on the full armor of God, have studied this text through different Bible Study, but I have never really understood them to their fullest extent until this Bible Study. <u>The Perfect Fit</u> explained each piece of the armor in scripture with wit, humor and detail that I had not heard before. It shows you how and when to put on that armor and get ready for battle. I now walk through my day fully armored instead of in defeat or out of God's will."

Karen G.   Clayton, NJ

Mona with soldier, Victoria.

Contact Mona Mauro

If you are interested in having Mona share with your group at a retreat, luncheon, seminar or to kick off "The Perfect Fit", she would be honored.

Please contact her at: Mona Mauro, 1805 Maple St, Newfield, NJ 08344.
monamauro@comcast.net, on Facebook,
or at her website: monamauro.com.

CPSIA information can be obtained
at www.ICGtesting.com
Printed in the USA
FSOW03n1505091116
27180FS